First Edition: 2024.

AF407057

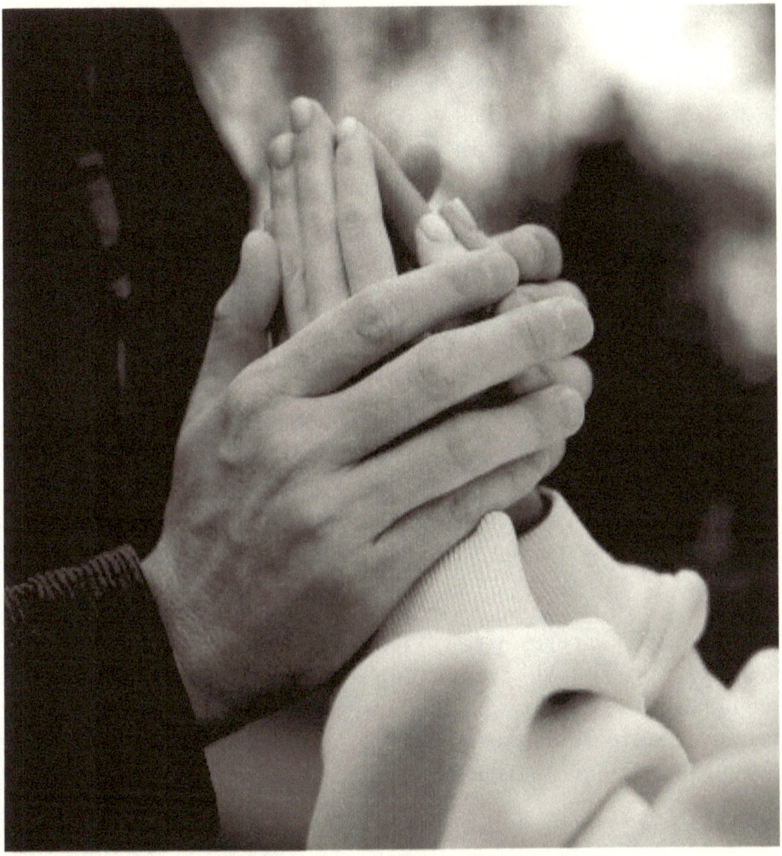

Published By: LOSD Publishing House, United Kingdom
(https://losd.co.uk/publishing/)

FOREWORD

Forgiveness is a powerful human virtue that transcends cultural and personal boundaries, offering the potential to heal and transform lives. In "The Book On Forgiveness," twenty-seven remarkable individuals share their deeply personal journeys of forgiveness in 24 chapters within the year 2024. Their stories, filled with honesty and courage, demonstrate the resilience of the human spirit and the profound impact that forgiveness can have.

The experiences in this book range from overcoming personal betrayals and familial conflicts to navigating professional disappointments and societal injustices. Each author reveals how forgiveness has been a transformative force in their lives, illustrating that it is not just a gift we give to others, but a liberating act for ourselves.

Forgiveness requires courage and vulnerability. It involves confronting our deepest wounds and making the conscious decision to let go of anger and resentment. This process, though challenging, leads to a sense of freedom and peace. Many of the authors also touch on the crucial aspect of self-forgiveness, learning to extend compassion to themselves as well as others.

As you read these pages, you will encounter stories of incredible strength and resilience. You will see how forgiveness has enabled individuals to rebuild their lives, restore relationships, and find renewed purpose. These narratives serve as a beacon of hope, challenging us to embrace the healing potential of forgiveness.

We hope that "The Book On Forgiveness" will inspire and guide you on your own journey of forgiveness, helping you find peace and liberation. Thank you for joining us on this transformative journey. May the wisdom and experiences shared in this book lead you to a life filled with compassion, understanding, and forgiveness.

DEDICATION

This book is dedicated to all those who have faced the challenging path of forgiveness. To those who have found the courage to forgive, to those still seeking it, and to those who have experienced the profound healing that forgiveness brings.

May your journey be guided by love, compassion, and the unwavering belief in the power of forgiveness to transform our world. To the unsung heroes who have silently borne the burden of pain and yet chosen to let go, and to those who continue to struggle with the decision to forgive, this book is for you.

Your strength and resilience are an inspiration. We also dedicate this book to future generations, hoping that they may grow in a world where forgiveness is understood, valued, and practiced as a cornerstone of human interaction and personal peace.

PROLOGUE

Forgiveness is more than an act; it is a journey that requires courage, strength, and an open heart. It is about letting go of past hurts, embracing compassion, and allowing ourselves to heal. The journey of forgiveness is often fraught with emotional turmoil, yet it is through this process that we find our true selves.

Within these twenty-four chapters in the year 2024, authors from diverse backgrounds share their personal journeys and insights on forgiveness. Each story is a testament to the transformative power of letting go and moving forward. These narratives span various experiences; from overcoming personal betrayals and familial conflicts to navigating professional disappointments, health challenges and societal injustices.

As you read these pages, you will discover the myriad ways in which forgiveness can change lives, mend relationships, and foster personal growth. Our hope is that these stories will inspire you to embark on your own path of forgiveness, finding peace and renewal along the way. May these accounts of resilience and grace serve as a guide and a source of strength as you navigate your own challenges and triumphs in the pursuit of forgiveness.

MESSAGE FROM LOSD

Welcome to "The Book On Forgiveness," a transformative collection of personal journeys that underscores the profound impact of forgiveness on our lives. At LOSD Publishing House, we are honoured to bring you this compilation of powerful, each one a testament to the resilience and strength of the human spirit.

LOSD Publishing House is proud to be one of the seven initiatives under the London Organisation of Skills Development (LOSD). Our mission is to 'illuminate minds and transform lives' through our publishing and writing services. We are dedicated to providing a platform for voices that inspire, educate, and foster a deeper understanding of the world.

In addition to LOSD Publishing, our initiatives include:

1. **Global Research Conferences & Global Research Journal:** Opportunities to Present your research. *'Ignite Your Passion For Sharing Research'*

2. **LOSD Publishing:** Publishing & writing services. *'Illuminate Minds & Transform Lives'*

3. **SkillFlex:** LOSD Online Courses (Digital assert) *'Empowering Learning for the Modern World'*

4. **SkillCast:** LOSD Podcast. *'Elevating Minds, Igniting Potential'*

5. **LOSD Skills Live:** Short Powerful Talk. *'Inspiring Ideas, Transforming Minds'*

6. **LOSD Excellence Awards:** Recognising Individuals &

   Organisations. *'Empowering Excellence: Igniting Paths to Success'*

7. **LOSD Business Wellbeing Retreat:** *'Find Your Balance & Unleash Success'*

MESSAGE FROM LOSD

Through these diverse initiatives, LOSD is committed to fostering a global community of learners, thinkers, and leaders. We hope "The Book On Forgiveness" will inspire you to embrace forgiveness and find peace and renewal in your own life.

Warm regards,

LOSD Publishing House United Kingdom

www.losd.co.uk

EDITOR'S MESSAGE

It has been an honour to edit "The Book On Forgiveness." This collection of narratives and insights are a powerful reminder of the healing potential inherent in the act of forgiveness. Each author's journey is unique, yet they all share a common thread of resilience and hope. The stories contained within these pages reflect a diverse array of experiences and perspectives, each offering valuable insights into the process and power of forgiveness.

We have been deeply moved by the stories shared within these pages and are grateful to each contributor for their willingness to be strong and authentic. Their bravery in sharing such personal experiences is a gift to all who read this book. Our desire is that this book will serve as hope and a source of strength for anyone seeking to forgive and heal. Through these stories, we aim to foster a greater understanding of forgiveness and its transformative impact, encouraging readers to embrace forgiveness in their own lives and, in turn, contribute to a more compassionate and understanding world.

Best wishes

Prof. Parin Somani & Martha Davidson

ACKNOWLEDGEMENTS

This book would not have been possible without the contributions of many individuals. We extend our deepest gratitude to the twenty-seven authors who shared their heartfelt stories and lessons on forgiveness within twenty-four chapters. Your courage and honesty are truly inspiring, and your willingness to be vulnerable has added immense value to this collection.

We also thank our families and friends for their unwavering support and encouragement throughout this journey. Your belief in the power of forgiveness and your constant encouragement have been our pillars of strength.

Finally, we thank our readers for embarking on this journey with us. May you find the inspiration and strength to embrace forgiveness in your own lives. Your openness to these stories and your willingness to reflect on them are what make this book truly meaningful.

BOOK DESCRIPTION

"The Book On Forgiveness" is a compelling anthology that brings together the voices of twenty-seven individuals who have faced the challenges of forgiveness. Each of the twenty-four chapters provides a unique perspective, offering insights into the significance of forgiveness, personal experiences that illustrate its power, lessons learned along the way, and advice to inspire others within the modern world.

This book is a testament to the transformative power of forgiveness and a guide for those seeking to embark on their own journey of healing. Through these narratives, readers will find encouragement, wisdom, and the profound realisation that forgiveness is a path to personal freedom and growth.

Each author shares a specific story, insights or a moment related to forgiveness, providing a candid glimpse into their journey. Authors reflect on the insights gained from their experiences, offering readers valuable lessons on the nature of forgiveness. In addition, each chapter concludes with advice and inspirational messages, aiming to inspire readers to embrace forgiveness in their own lives.

This collection of stories is not just about forgiving others but also about self-forgiveness and the profound impact it can have on personal well-being and relationships. "The Book On Forgiveness" is an invaluable resource for anyone looking to understand the multifaceted nature of forgiveness and its power to heal and transform.

CONTENTS

INTRODUCTION

The authors in this book have made an important discovery: to forgive is to set a prisoner free and discover that the prisoner was you. There are no happy people in a bitter marriage, family, or circle of friends. If you want to live a joyful life, you must forgive yourself, as well as others. Once you have forgiven someone who has lifted a great burden of anger and resentment from your shoulders, you will find peace and contentment replacing those negative feelings. You will breathe easier, smile more often, sleep better, and literally walk lighter. The solution is there for all those who choose to take it: forgiveness.

These people at one time thought it was impossible to forgive. Some thought it was necessary to hate; some refused to forgive someone who was no longer living. Yet in all instances, scales fell from their eyes, their hearts opened, and through forgiveness, they freed not only their wrongdoer but themselves as well. These are ordinary people who have been bathed in grace. They can inspire you. They can serve you as an example. All of their stories are true: many of them are ongoing. Some problems can be solved in a moment, but most take time. But even a challenging love can be handled with love, and forgiveness is the key. We are blessed to have the opportunity to read their heartfelt words and benefit from their insights, learnings and be inspiration.

CHAPTER 1

FORGIVENESS

And Unconscious

AWARENESS

Martha Davidson

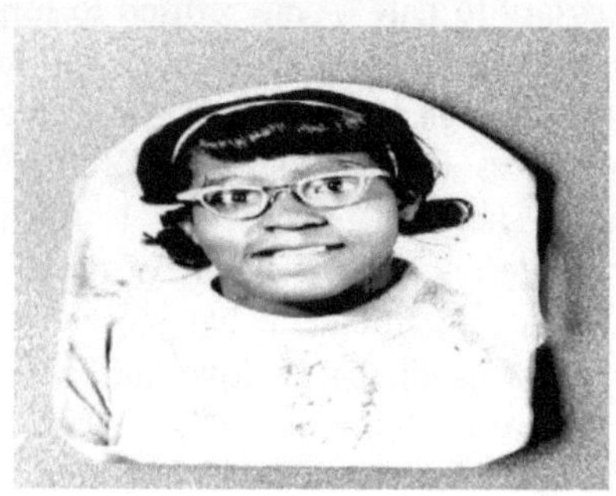

As I reflect on forgiveness and its power, I begin to ask myself: have I ever considered forgiveness for my unknown early childhood? Reflecting on this perspective, I begin to have a profound awakening. Without the forgiveness of the unknown experiences that left me disconnected, lonely, rejected, and experiencing selective mutism, would forgiveness of the unknown create a new reality, releasing stored memories and unreleased trauma? By choosing to forgive whatever happened to me, I realise I can create a space for me to become who I came here to become.

This realisation washes over me like a warm wave, both comforting and challenging. I find myself standing at the edge of a vast, misty field. Six weathered stone markers rise from the ground, each representing one of the foster homes I lived in before age six. The mist swirls around them, obscuring their details – much like my memories of that time.

As I gaze at these markers, I feel a familiar weight settle over me. It's as if I'm wearing an invisible backpack, filled with the accumulated impact of disconnection, rejection, aggression, and loneliness from those early years. The straps dig into my shoulders, a constant reminder of the burdens I've carried for so long.

"It's time," I say to myself, my voice barely above a whisper. "Time to forgive the unknown, to release what I can't fully remember."

I take a deep breath and step into the misty field. As I approach the first marker, I'm reminded of a locked box without a key. I know something important is inside, but I can't access it. This is the nature of my early memories – present but obscured, influencing my life in ways I can't fully grasp.

"How do I forgive what I can't remember?" I wonder aloud.

As if in response, a gentle breeze stirs the mist, and I hear a whisper: "Forgiveness isn't about unlocking the box. It's about acknowledging its presence and choosing to move forward anyway."

This insight settles over me like a warm blanket. I realise that forgiving the unknown isn't about uncovering every detail of my past. It's about accepting that these experiences happened and choosing to release their hold on me.

I place my hand on the first stone marker, feeling its rough texture beneath my palm. "I acknowledge you," I say. "Even though I can't see you clearly, I know you've been part of my journey."

As I speak, I feel a slight loosening of the invisible backpack. It's a small shift, but it gives me the courage to continue.

Moving to the second marker, I'm struck by another metaphor. My early experiences are like the roots of a tree – hidden beneath the surface but profoundly influencing my growth. Some of these roots have nourished me, helping me develop resilience and strength. Others have twisted and constrained me, limiting my ability to flourish fully.

"Forgiveness," I realise, "is like being a conscious gardener. I can't dig up all the roots, but I can choose which ones to nurture and which ones to gently prune."

With this understanding, I address the second marker: "I choose to nurture the strength these experiences have given me, while releasing the constraints they've placed on my growth."

The mist swirls again, and I feel another slight lightening of my burden.

As I approach the third marker, I think about my brain and how these early experiences have shaped my neural pathways. I imagine my mind as a vast city, with some roads well-travelled and others less so. The experiences from my foster care years have created highways of fear, doubt, and self-protection – paths my thoughts automatically travel when triggered.

But standing here, facing this marker of my past, I realise I have the power to create new roads. Forgiveness, in this context, is like being a city planner. I can't demolish the old highways overnight, but I can start building new ones – pathways of self-love, trust, and openness.

"I choose to create new neural pathways," I declare to the marker. "I'm paving roads of forgiveness and self-compassion."

As I speak, I feel a tingling sensation throughout my body, as if my very cells are responding to this decision.

The fourth marker brings to mind the image of a radio. My early experiences are like static, interfering with the clear broadcast of my true self. This static has made it hard for me to tune into my authentic voice, to hear the music of my soul clearly.

Forgiveness, I realise, is like fine-tuning the radio. It doesn't eliminate the static entirely, but it allows me to hear my true frequency more clearly.

"I'm adjusting my inner dial," I say to the marker. "I'm tuning into the frequency of my highest self, even if there's still some static in the background."

As I make this declaration, I notice the mist starting to thin slightly. The markers are still obscured, but the air around me feels clearer.

Approaching the fifth marker, I think about how my unknown past has been like a lens through which I've viewed the world. This lens, smudged by the fingerprints of disconnection and pain, has often distorted my perception, making it hard to see situations and relationships clearly.

Forgiveness, in this analogy, is like carefully cleaning that lens. It doesn't change what happened in the past, but it allows me to see the present and future with greater clarity.

"I'm wiping clean the lens of my perception," I tell the fifth marker. "I choose to see myself and the world around me with compassion and clarity."

As I speak these words, I feel a shift in my vision. The world around me seems brighter, more vibrant, as if a veil has been lifted.

I take a step back, looking at all six markers. They're still there, still partially obscured by mist, but they no longer feel oppressive or limiting. Instead, they stand as monuments to my resilience, my journey, and my growth.

In a clear, strong voice, I address the field and myself: "I forgive the unknown circumstances that led to my foster care experiences. I forgive those who may have caused pain, even if I can't remember their faces. I forgive myself for the ways I've held onto this pain. I release the impact of disconnection, rejection, aggressiveness, and loneliness."

As I speak these words, something remarkable happens. The mist begins to glow, transforming from a grey haze into a shimmering, golden light. This light surrounds me, infusing every cell of my body with warmth and energy.

I close my eyes, basking in this glow, and find myself transported to a new mental landscape. Here, I see my unconscious mind as a vast, underground cavern. For years, this cavern has been filled with shadows – the unremembered experiences of my early years casting dark shapes on the walls.

But now, as I bring the light of forgiveness into this space, something transformative occurs. The shadows don't disappear entirely, but they begin to dance and shift. What once seemed menacing now appears almost beautiful – a complex interplay of light and dark that tells the story of my journey.

The Book On Forgiveness

I realise that forgiving the unknown isn't about erasing these shadows. It's about bringing light into the cavern, allowing me to see the beauty and complexity of my whole self – including the parts shaped by unseen forces.

As this understanding washes over me, I feel a surge of energy coursing through my body. It's as if every cell is realigning, shedding old patterns and embracing new possibilities. I recognise this as the unleashing of my true potential – the light I came here to be, finally freed from the constraints of my unknown past.

Back in the misty field, I open my eyes. The six markers are still there, but they've transformed. Instead of weathered stone, they now appear to be made of crystal, each one refracting the golden light in unique and beautiful ways.

I understand now that my early experiences, even those I can't fully remember, have contributed to the person I am. They've given me depth, complexity, and a unique perspective on the world. By forgiving the unknown, I haven't erased these experiences – I've transmuted them into sources of strength and wisdom.

"I am now free to be who I came here to be," I declare, my voice ringing with certainty. "My past has shaped me, but it no longer defines me. I step into my highest potential, unburdened by the unknown."

As these words leave my lips, I feel a final, powerful release. The last vestiges of the invisible backpack fall away, and I stand taller, lighter, more authentically myself than ever before.

The misty field begins to fade around me, replaced by a vast, open landscape filled with infinite possibilities. I feel a deep sense of peace, purpose, and potential.

I take a step forward, then another. With each step, I feel more aligned with my true self. The journey of forgiveness has released me from the shadows of my past, allowing my inner light to shine fully in the world.

As I walk into my future, I carry with me the wisdom of my experiences, the strength of my resilience, and the unlimited potential of a heart opened by forgiveness. I am ready to write the next chapters of my story, free from the constraints of the past, fully embracing who I came here to be.

The slight remembrances of the past have served their purpose. Now, they fade into the background, allowing my true self to step fully into the light. My unconscious mind, once a cavern of shadows, is now a wellspring of creativity, intuition, and power.

I move forward with confidence, my entire being aligned with my highest potential. The unknown aspects of my past no longer hold me back – instead, they've become the fertile soil from which my brightest future can grow.

As I continue on my path, I realise that forgiveness is not a one-time event, but an ongoing process. There may be moments when the mist tries to creep back in, when old patterns attempt to reassert themselves. But now I have the tools, the understanding, and the inner light to navigate these challenges.

I am the author of my own story, the captain of my own ship, the gardener of my own mind. The unknown parts of my past have given me a unique perspective, a depth of understanding that I can now use to illuminate the way for others who may be struggling with their own unseen burdens.

My journey of forgiving the unknown has not only freed me but has also given me a gift to share with the world. My light, now unobscured, has the power to inspire, to heal, to transform.

As I stand on the threshold of my bright future, I make one final declaration to myself and to the universe: "I am the light I came here to be. My past is a part of me, but it does not control me. I move forward in forgiveness, in power, in purpose. I am free."

With these words, I step fully into my power, ready to shine my light in all its brilliance. The unknown has been acknowledged, forgiven, and integrated. Now, it's time to live the life I was always meant to live – unburdened, unafraid, and utterly, gloriously free.

The Book On Forgiveness

About the Author:

Martha Davidson is a neuro-leadership consultant and advocate for women in leadership, distils her personal journey into powerful strategies for resilience and empowerment. Her expertise fuels a unique approach to overcoming the challenges women face in STEM leadership roles. A renowned international speaker and author, Davidson's 25 years of leadership experience inform her work at Mpowering Minds Now, where she equips aspiring female executives to transcend mid-level management. Martha Davidson Visionary Global Women Leadership Network Transform Leadership Impossibilities into Possibilities.

CHAPTER 2

EMBRACING

FORGIVENES:

A Journey Of Healing & Compassion

Prof. Dr. Parin Somani

Forgiveness has been a foundation of my personal and professional journey, a profound force that has reshaped my perspective, healed deep wounds, and inspired me to cultivate empathy and understanding in all aspects of life. Through my experiences, I have learned that forgiveness is not just a gift we give to others but a transformative act that liberates the soul and fosters profound personal growth.

The Significance of Forgiveness

Forgiveness, to me, is a profound act of liberation, a conscious decision to release the grip of anger, resentment, and pain. It is a journey towards healing and reconciliation, both within us and in our relationships with others. My exploration of forgiveness has been deeply intertwined with moments of personal challenge and triumph, each experience shaping my understanding of its transformative power.

My Turning Point in Forgiveness

One pivotal moment that profoundly influenced my perspective on forgiveness was when I temporarily lost my vision, endured life-threatening aggressive cancer twice, suffered from Covid-19, and experienced a mini-stroke. These series of health crises shook me to my core, challenging not only my physical resilience but also testing the depths of my emotional and spiritual strength.

The temporary loss of my vision was a stark reminder of life's fragility, a moment where darkness enveloped my world, both literally and figuratively. It was a period of profound vulnerability and fear, where I grappled with the uncertainty of whether I would ever see again. In those moments of darkness, I found solace in faith and the unwavering support of my loved ones, who became my pillars of strength. Fortunately through an intense course of steroid treatment I regained my vision. But, I also acquired unwanted weight going from a UK size 10 to 24 which led to another battle. Having been in the media, physical appearance had always been an important component of fitting in with societal norms. It was time this changed, I thought to myself, I was just grateful for my life

Enduring aggressive cancer twice compounded this experience, thrusting me into a relentless battle for survival. The treatments were gruelling, testing my endurance and challenging my resolve on a daily basis. Each round of chemotherapy, each surgery, was a stark reminder of the fragility of life and the preciousness of each moment. Despite the physical toll, it was the emotional and spiritual journey through forgiveness that became equally, if not more, demanding.

Facing Covid-19 added yet another layer of uncertainty and fear. The pandemic swept across the globe, affecting millions, and I found myself confronting the virus. It was a time where isolation became both a necessity and a metaphor for the internal struggle to find peace and acceptance. It was a moment of profound reflection, where forgiveness emerged not just as an act towards others, but towards myself to forgive my body for its frailties, to forgive the circumstances that led to all these health crises I have endured, and to find a path forward with renewed purpose and determination.

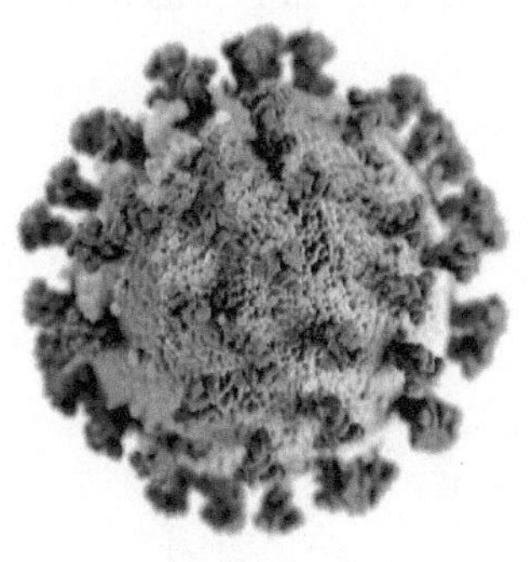

Insights from the Journey of Forgiveness

Through these profound challenges, forgiveness became my lifeline. It was not a single act but a continuous process, a journey of letting go of anger, resentment, and self-blame. Forgiving those who unknowingly contributed to my suffering, forgiving myself for moments of weakness or doubt, and ultimately, finding compassion amidst adversity. This journey reshaped my perspective on forgiveness in profound ways. It taught me that forgiveness is not a sign of weakness, but of strength, a courageous choice to transcend pain and embrace healing. It allowed me to release the burdens of anger and bitterness, paving the way for inner peace and resilience. Through forgiveness, I found the strength to focus on what truly matters, living each day with gratitude, compassion, and a profound appreciation for the gift of life.

The Emotional Liberation

Forgiveness is a multifaceted process, deeply intertwined with our emotions and mental state. It requires us to confront our pain, anger, and disappointment head-on. In doing so, we open ourselves to emotional liberation, shedding the heavy burden of negative

emotions that can cloud our judgment and hinder our growth. When I faced my health crises, I was initially overwhelmed by a wave of emotions, fear, anger, and a deep sense of injustice.

But as I began to embrace forgiveness, I felt a gradual lightening of this emotional weight. Forgiveness allowed me to process these feelings, understand their origins, and ultimately, let them go. This emotional liberation was pivotal in my healing journey, helping me to cultivate a more positive and hopeful outlook on life.

The Mental Shift

Forgiveness also necessitates a significant mental shift. It involves changing our perception of those who have wronged us, and sometimes, of ourselves. This mental transformation is not about condoning the wrongs done but about seeing them through a lens of compassion and understanding. It is about recognising the humanity in others and in ourselves, acknowledging that we all make mistakes and that holding onto grudges only perpetuates our suffering. My journey through illness required me to forgive myself for my body's perceived failures. This mental shift was not easy; it demanded introspection and a willingness to challenge my negative self-talk. However, it was through this mental reorientation that I found peace and acceptance, allowing me to move forward with a clearer and more compassionate mindset.

The Spiritual Reawakening

On a spiritual level, forgiveness is a profound act of faith and surrender. It involves trusting in a higher power, believing in the inherent goodness of people, and understanding that there is a greater purpose behind our struggles. For me,

this spiritual aspect of forgiveness was a beacon of hope during my darkest times. My faith provided me with strength and comfort, guiding me through the complexities of my health challenges. By embracing forgiveness, I experienced a spiritual reawakening, a renewed sense of purpose, and a deeper connection with the divine. This spiritual journey reinforced my belief in the transformative power of forgiveness and its ability to heal and uplift the soul.

The Ripple Effect of Forgiveness

Healing Relationships

Forgiveness has a remarkable ripple effect, extending beyond personal healing to mend and strengthen relationships. It fosters empathy and understanding, enabling us to connect with others on a deeper level. In my professional and personal life, embracing forgiveness has transformed my interactions and relationships. It has allowed me to approach conflicts with a more open heart and mind, leading to resolutions that are rooted in compassion and mutual respect. Forgiveness has also helped me to build a supportive network of individuals who share my values and aspirations, enhancing my ability to contribute positively to the lives of others.

Inspiring Others

My journey of forgiveness has also served as an inspiration to others. By sharing my experiences and the lessons I have learned, I hope to encourage others to embrace forgiveness as a pathway to healing and growth. Through my work as a speaker and author, I have had the privilege of reaching a diverse audience, sharing the transformative power of forgiveness and its impact on my life. It is my belief that by fostering a culture of forgiveness, we can create a more compassionate and harmonious world, where individuals are empowered to overcome their struggles and thrive.

The Book On Forgiveness

Practical Steps that have helped me to Embrace Forgiveness

Self-Reflection and Awareness

The first step towards forgiveness is self-reflection and awareness. It involves taking a deep and honest look at our emotions and identifying the sources of our pain and resentment. This process requires courage and vulnerability, as it often brings to the surface difficult and uncomfortable feelings. However, it is through this introspective journey that we can begin to understand and address our emotional wounds. For me, self-reflection was a crucial part of my healing process. It allowed me to acknowledge my pain, confront my fears, and ultimately, find the strength to forgive.

Compassion and Empathy

Cultivating compassion and empathy is essential in the journey of forgiveness. It involves putting ourselves in the shoes of others, understanding their perspectives, and recognising their humanity. This empathetic approach helps to soften our hearts and open our minds to the possibility of forgiveness. In my experiences, empathy played a pivotal role in my ability to forgive. By understanding the struggles and motivations of those who had wronged me, I was able to see them in a new light, which facilitated the process of forgiveness.

Letting Go of Anger and Resentment

Forgiveness requires us to let go of anger and resentment, which are often the biggest obstacles to healing. Holding onto these negative emotions can keep us trapped in a cycle of pain and bitterness, preventing us from moving forward. Letting go does not mean forgetting or excusing the wrongs done to us, but rather, choosing to release the hold these emotions have on our lives. Through my journey, I learned that letting go is a gradual process that requires patience and persistence. It involves actively working to replace negative thoughts with positive ones and seeking peace and understanding in place of anger.

Seeking Support

The journey of forgiveness can be challenging, and it is important to seek support from others. This support can come from friends, family, mentors, or professionals who can provide guidance and encouragement. During my health crises, the support of my loved ones was invaluable. Their unwavering faith in my ability to overcome my challenges and their constant encouragement gave me the strength to keep going. Surrounding ourselves with a supportive network can make the journey of forgiveness more manageable and less isolating.

Practicing Forgiveness Daily

Forgiveness is not a one-time event but a continuous practice. It involves making a daily commitment to let go of negative emotions and to approach life with a forgiving heart. This practice can be incorporated into our daily routines through mindfulness, meditation, and positive affirmations. By consistently practicing forgiveness, we can cultivate a more compassionate and resilient mindset. In my own life, daily practices of mindfulness and gratitude have been instrumental inmaintaining a forgiving attitude. They have helped me to stay focused on the positive aspects of life and to approach challenges with grace and understanding.

Inspiring Others through Forgiveness

My journey of forgiveness has been a profound and transformative experience, shaping my perspective on life and guiding me towards personal and professional growth. Through my experiences, I have come to understand that forgiveness is not a sign of weakness but a powerful act of strength and compassion. It has allowed me to heal, to find inner peace, and to live each day with a sense of gratitude and purpose.

By sharing my journey, I hope to inspire others to embrace forgiveness as a pathway to healing and renewal. I believe that by fostering a culture of forgiveness, we can create a world where wounds are healed, relationships are restored, and individuals thrive in harmony and mutual respect. Through forgiveness, we can build a more compassionate and understanding society, where everyone has the opportunity to reach their true potential.

In my work as a speaker, author, and advocate for education, women empowerment, and youth development, I strive to promote the values of forgiveness and compassion. I am committed to encouraging others to embark on their own journeys of forgiveness, to overcome their challenges, and to achieve their dreams. By working together, we can create positive global change and build a brighter future for all.

Forgiveness is a journey, not a destination. It is a continuous process of letting go, healing, and growing. It requires patience, persistence, and a deep commitment to self-awareness and compassion. But through this journey, we can find liberation, peace, and a profound sense of fulfilment. From experience I believe that by embracing forgiveness, and you will discover a world of healing and endless possibility.

About the Author:

Prof. Dr. Parin Somani is CEO and Director of LOSD (www.losd.co.uk), a distinguished Academic Scholar, three times TEDx Speaker, and Author of 21 books. To inspire individuals to reach their true potential, she has won Mrs. Universe 2022, Mrs. World 2022 in Thailand, Mrs. BritAsian 2021 in London, Mrs. India 2021, Mrs. Universe International 2021, and Mrs. India Global 2021. She has been recognised in numerous World Record Books like the Guinness World Records and was one of the Lead Editors of 'The Thickest Book in the World.' Her passion for lifelong learning and helping global societies has led her to achieve 2 Academic and 6 Honorary Doctorates and numerous multi-international awards. She is immensely grateful for all her honours, and she has been invited to deliver keynote speeches at conferences at Cambridge, Harvard and Oxford University, and many more. Her global travels to 127 countries have enabled her to contribute to her main areas of focus: education, women empowerment, and youth development.

CHAPTER 3

CHALLENGES

AND SOCIETY

Parveen Smith

Forgiveness is a topic that comes into realisation every time something happens to a person who cannot let go, we know many experiences will affect forgiveness. Is it easy to forgive?

I have overcome many challenges and I have had to go through forgiveness, and I celebrate today as a triumphant era. I will share concepts and everyone will have their own thoughts. Experiences do shape us, and I know what shaped me.

Forgiveness, as defined by Wikipedia, is the intentional and voluntary process by which a person who may feel wronged, victimised, harmed, or hurt, undergoes a change in feelings and attitude towards an offender, and overcomes negative emotions such as resentment and the desire for vengeance.

As a person who has faced a lot of adversity, I would like you to keep an open mind on this subject matter as I will share certain scenarios.

Challenges From Childhood

When faced with life's many challenges, we may ponder whether to forgive and forget or to harbour grudges. The decision often hinges on the nature of the events. For instance, when parents separate or divorce, should we cling to blame, on one or the other parent? Or should we examine the behaviours that led to the escalation and outcome of events? I believe that at some point, particularly from a child's perspective, one learns to accept the separation or divorce, as hard as it may be at that time, the adjustment happens to continue with life, understanding that it is the reality and striving to move forward is better.

It's true that children often have a remarkable ability to adapt and move forward in various situations. Their innocence and openness can make them quick to forgive and accept apologies, allowing them to adjust more easily. This resilience is one of the many wonderful aspects of childhood.

As one grows into their teenage and adult years, the frequency of seeing separated or divorced parents may vary. These experiences can shape an adult's understanding that such events can happen to anyone, emphasising the importance of cherishing life's precious moments.

Reflection on one's upbringing might lead to a resolve to improve upon the aspects one disliked in their parent's relationship. Learning from their parents' situation and circumstances, one might reach a point of forgiveness, accepting that their parents were not suited for each other due to irreconcilable differences or conflicts. This is where we might choose to 'let it be' and move on. It's a realisation that we may come to embrace as part of our growth. As a person matures, they will see how their life shaped them and then to realise that it was beneficial for parents to go their separate ways to bring a more harmonious outcome to all involved.

Teenagers often rebel against their parents due to a lack of understanding, or because hormonal changes may be overwhelming. The transition from adolescence to adulthood is a significant journey that we have all experienced, and we know it can be challenging at times. This rebellion can sometimes cause issues in evolving societies and the futures we are heading towards. Nurturing young people and having meaningful and regular communication can help.

It is my belief that only when we become parents ourselves, do we fully comprehend the challenges of childhood. We can then reflect on our upbringing and maybe the hardships we faced. If a person has endured a difficult childhood, they might assign blame, as they revisit their past through recurring dreams or nightmares, leading to sleepless nights filled with questions about their experiences. This can significantly impact an individual's mental and emotional well-being. As and when possible, it would be beneficial to seek the appropriate expertise support.

From childhood to adolescence, and eventually into parenthood, we traverse life's journey, only truly understanding the parental experience when we have children of our own and face life's challenges.

"Forgiveness is not an occasional act; it is a constant attitude." - Martin Luther King, Jr.

Anger And Forgiveness

I will share my personal story. As an adult, particularly after having three children, one begins to comprehend the true essence of forgiveness. I have had a difficult path to endure, and I could have been angry all of my life but I chose to move forward with less resentment as possible every single time. I often talked about my challenges with my husband and family. Memories would surface and at times I found it difficult especially when my father died as my parents separated in my early years. In my recent adult years, it was a very intense time, as the memories and thoughts brought up sadness that I did not get to say goodbye. He passed away all alone. He did not have any family members at his funeral. This was like a sword had pierced my heart. My few memories arose, and I was filled with anger not towards my father but to the situation where I didn't know where he was and he died alone. As I am a celebrant and conducted funerals this was a hard pill to swallow. I did not need to forgive my father. I accepted his choices. I was having to forgive myself for feeling angry in this situation, this time also made me question many things. This period alone took 18 months to heal.

It becomes possible to release the anger or begin healing from the resentment held towards a family member or friend. Clinging to negative emotions only causes distress to our own soul. As individuals, we often suffer more from holding onto resentment than the person it is directed towards. This is because we cannot fully grasp what the other person is feeling; they have their own issues and reasons for their actions. Holding onto anger only creates disharmony within us, leading to an imbalance in our body system and misalignment of our chakras. The failure to address and heal these feelings over time only compounds the difficulty. So, letting go, forgiving, and healing oneself is paramount for moving forward. We must release past hurts, even though it may be challenging, especially when anger stems from unresolved issues. Understanding that harbouring resentment harms our well-being as much as it does the other person, it is crucial to see this point. Is it worth the suffering? Would it not be better to seek peace, closure, and forgiveness?

I firmly believe in the power of forgiveness, although I acknowledge it is not simple. Forgiveness is a process that requires the right mindset and a genuine desire to forgive the other person.

Already as we are looking into the stories from a child's point of view, heading towards adolescence and maybe having children, only then do we know what it is like to experience being a parent and going through hardships of life. Forgiveness is not an overnight turn around it takes time. I forgive everyone who has been part of my journey and who may have been unkind and caused me distress in extreme situations and circumstances and above all I am know it will help to heal me. I forgive myself also for any wrongdoing as I was part of that journey too. I also acknowledge that I am not perfect as no one is. I may have caused others to feel vulnerable and may have caused them emotional upsets through my voice. I accept this too, hence why I feel it is always important to self-forgive if we have caused some realised or unrealised hurt to others. Saying that we may realise that we are speaking up for the benefit of others, but they may not understand why we speak in a certain way. We are sometimes abrupt and straight to the point because we want to make an impact for things to improve for the person we care about.

If you want to see the brave, look to those who can return love for hatred. If you want to see the heroic, look to those who can forgive.

- Bhagavad Gita

Cultures And Societies

Reflecting on the history of wars, hurt, anger, and disruption on our planet, it's evident that such events have not benefited our future.

It's recognised that religion and ownership of land has often been a source of disharmony among cultures and societies. When people suffer and there is loss of lives, feelings of anger, revenge, blame, hurt, and an inability to forgive naturally arise.

In most cases, human society finds it challenging to forgive under these circumstances. Observing the destruction across our world, it becomes exceedingly difficult for leniency to those responsible for such crimes of destruction, and disharmony. The sight of war-ravaged places overwhelms us, making it hard to grasp the extent of the damage, forgiveness of the perpetrators, and understanding the loss of innocent lives can be tough and heart-breaking.

The scale of such devastation often defies comprehension and forgiveness. Many people choose to disengage from media coverage of these events, as it can be soul-crushing to witness and hear about such destruction.

When faced with tragedies of this magnitude, understanding, comprehending, and forgiving can seem impossible. Some may choose to shut themselves off or turn a blind eye to cope with the harsh reality. Many people are making choices to not listen to what is happening in our world because they are finding it difficult to comprehend and it is soul destroying. As some people are more sensitive to others, it is better to avoid such news articles.

Wrongs are often forgiven, but contempt never is. Our pride remembers it forever. Lord Chesterfield

Is Forgiveness Complex?

I believe the human soul is capable of forgiveness on a personal level. Personal forgiveness arises when someone has wronged you, causing disharmony in a relationship or work environment. It's a deeply personal decision to either live with the hurt or to forgive.

Hence, I believe the best way to move through life's traumas and tragedies is to strive for forgiveness. True forgiveness comes from a deep, soulful, and heartfelt place, allowing one to move forward.

When my sister passed away, I was engulfed in rage. At just 19, her loss devastated my family. My soul was overwhelmed with grief. Blame seemed inevitable, as she was found dead in her house. Nothing made sense, leading to a thorough investigation by the police and CID's. I still found it unbelievable. I couldn't sleep or find peace; it consumed me entirely. I wondered if it was my fault for not hearing her out, if I had missed something vital in our talks. These thoughts constantly taunted me. However, I believed she would have shared with me if something was wrong, as she had in past discussions. Our family was in disbelief over the tragedy of losing a 20-year-old with so much ahead of her, leaving behind her 18-month-old daughter. Again, as it was an intensely

sorrowful period for our family, beyond comprehension. We were in disbelief. As I share with you, how can one come to terms with such grief such shock, such trauma and even find forgiveness in this situation. On a personal soul

level, we would feel more at ease and at peace knowing we can forgive rather than holding on to past hurts.

So, I asked a gentleman can one forgive and this is what he said. "We already understand that forgiveness has different levels. For instance, we talked the other day about a man we all knew, his son had killed his mum, who had a serious conflict with his family and then he was in prison. Now, it seems he's back, talking to his dad and possibly even living with him, but his dad has let him in. Has his dad forgiven him, or just allowed him back into the house? Perhaps he's partly forgiven him because he is his son. The issue with forgiveness is that it's complicated by emotions, making it hard to let go. It's easier not to forgive someone who isn't related or known to you. People often say you can't move on until you've forgiven, right?"

Forgiveness can be a complex process, especially when the truth of what happened is unclear. It's natural to question whether you can truly forgive someone without knowing all the facts. Trust plays a significant role in forgiveness, and without clarity, it can be challenging to move forward. The question is indeed valid and reflects the difficulty of navigating forgiveness in uncertain situations. How do you feel about the idea of forgiving and cannot forgetting?

The concept of forgiveness is complex, especially in extreme circumstances. People often say they can forgive but not forget. For instance, if someone caused great harm, like taking a child's life, the affected may choose to forgive to move on, yet they'll never forget the incident. It's a personal journey where forgiving doesn't necessarily mean forgetting.

I know people who have lost their loved ones and situations occurred before their loved one passed away. There may not have been any forgiveness in these situations and that person can be left thinking they never had a resolve. In these situations, the individuals' memories, thoughts and emotions may never have peace of mind.

As I have spoken to some of these people, we discussed forgiveness could also be a deep karmic consequence. What has happened in the life lived may have some Karmic attachments.

The belief that our actions and experiences in life may carry karmic attachments may offer a sense of understanding and closure.

It's a profound topic that touches on the interconnectedness of our lives and the impact of our actions. How do you feel about the concept of karma and its influence on our lives?

Losing loved ones is incredibly difficult, and it's natural to reflect on the events that occurred before their passing. Many people find comfort in discussing forgiveness with their loved ones to put things into a peaceful situation.

Personality and background of the person do matter as the personality will show compassion and empathy. Some people are more forgiving than others and it may well link to the persons faith, culture and religion.

Forgiveness can indeed be challenging, especially for those who have grown up in environments where empathy and emotional expression were not nurtured. It's not always easy to forgive, particularly when the person who caused harm may not show remorse or understand the impact of their actions. Understanding someone's background and the factors that shaped their behaviour can sometimes open a path to forgiveness, but it's a complex and deeply personal process.

How do you think we can encourage more empathy and understanding in our communities?

Communication, nurturing, love and respect are key for the world. When there is harmony there will be less requirement for forgiveness.

The act of forgiveness is love for all. When the time is required to do so it will be appreciated.

The Book On Forgiveness

How people treat you is their karma; how you react is yours. Wayne Dyer

Some Thoughts:

Forgiving without forgetting is a complex issue. If there's no resolution, forgiveness can seem impossible.

Memories of the event may persist, suggesting forgiveness hasn't truly occurred.

Understanding the situation is overwhelming and still for some, their faith may make it easier to forgive.

Can one forgive if they cannot forget?

Some people do forgive to move forward.

It's a dilemma because the memory lingers. Some may choose to forgive to move forward, not allowing the past to hold them back, yet they won't forget the incident.

Forgetting means erasing the memory, which is impossible for significant events, like a murder. What I am highlighting is that forgiveness is a personal journey

The Book On Forgiveness

Some Tips To Help You:

Breathe through the situation and take a moment to reflect, what has just happened is it worth the imbalance in your own health?

Grieve from the situation and receive the healing.

Forgive when your heart and soul are in alignment.

Be gentle with yourself. Take time to look at the situation, make your own decision if you should forgive.

In every little situation when you feel in your heart you have made a mistake then say sorry and forgive yourself and the other person.

Let go of any doubt and fear.

Receive healing regularly.

Accept and appreciate yourself, just as you are. Your self-love and confidence shine through to inspire others, while reminding yourself that you are worthy and valuable.

When you run into an obstacle or unexpected problem, take a deep breath. Out loud, tell yourself, "I'm not going to let this stop my progress. I'll come up with a solution and continue on."

Wouldn't it be amazing to be in a world of less conflict and the reasons for forgiveness.

"The weak can never forgive. Forgiveness is the attribute of the strong." - Mahatma Gandhi

About the Author:

Parveen Smith is a transformative coach and global speaker, has an inspiring journey that promotes transformation. With over two decades of expertise, she is a recognised authority in her field and the author of three books. Parveen Smith's influence reaches beyond coaching; she has taught in schools, presented assemblies on culture, diversity, and emotional well-being, and has been honoured with numerous awards for her contributions in recent years.

CHAPTER 4

EMBRACING MOTIONAL PAIN

Dr Anjula Murmu

Pain is an inevitable part of life. It might be physical or emotional. Emotional pain usually involves other people. People might deceive us, cheat on us, or physically hurt us in numerous ways. These are the things we try to avoid. Avoiding pain will lead us to guard our hearts at the expense of connecting to others. Emotional pain happens even with positive relationships. We never want to hurt a loved one, but it can happen by accident. How do we manage the inevitable pain from these relationships? What response makes the most sense and will heal and strengthen relationships and help us form more meaningful connections in the future?

The importance of forgiveness in personal growth

Forgiveness is a very valuable personal trait necessary for good mental health and personal growth, not only from the perspective of a mature individual but also in the context of personal and social well-being, and as a necessary virtue for a successful and satisfying human existence. Forgiving injury or insult is a necessary personal attitude and moral virtue. The New Testament, informing the teachings of the Bible, especially in the Gospel of the New Testament, has termed it as the heart of Christian doctrine. From a religious perspective, God forgives us, and we should, in turn, forgive others. We should do unto others as God does unto us. Yet forgiving in relationships, practicing forgiveness, asks something of us that can be a high price to pay. When we open ourselves to being forgiving, it is important that we first face the reality of the pain caused by the injury or renouncing the reasoning "bad" of the anger that causes real pain, rather than forgetting about the whole event or denying the intensity of the wound.

The problem with this, when it comes to forgiving others, is that there may be a risk that we cross over to a position where forgiving feels "silly" in situations where, in fact, it would be wrong to forgive.

To forgive, therefore, necessitates a weighing of the intensity of the experience inflicted in light of the intensity of the pain, accepting the injury as being part of the life of relationships, and renouncing the vision of anger as being "all bad," and also balancing this by the necessity of the victim where persons are injured in different ways and threatened in different degrees.

Personal Experience

I see the healing power of forgiveness every day. It hastens recovery. It lowers blood pressure and other key risk factors for heart disease. But my daily experience with the power of forgiveness is not a reason that the theme was chosen for our lecture, at least not directly. Instead, it was selected in order to confront us with those aspects of our soul, our brokenness, our values in society as a whole and as individuals that are at a loss. What is our attitude when we, or others, break the trust that is based on our deepest values towards one another? In the interplay of forgiveness and justice, a wide range of questions on social, ethical and moral aspects related to human nature become obvious: These aspects are truly important, but not within the scope of my lecture.

So, I will not refer to one of those but rather convey my personal experiences with forgiveness to you. To this end, I would like to focus mostly on a personal reflection of forgiveness in authentic personal stories of fellow human beings, stories that have inspired me for numerous years and that have greatly influenced my professional career; partially motivated me to pursue it as well. Be aware that these stories demand our attention and engagement for the true challenging and difficult questions associated with them. When you read the title of my lecture, "Personal reflections on forgiveness: Lessons learned and inspiring journeys," or listen to the introduction of a speech in which a doctor is invited to speak about something like "the healing power of forgiveness," you might wonder about connections to clinical practice. After all, the medical humanities should provide knowledge and experiences that ultimately are useful to healthcare professionals and those who are affected by illness.

Sharing a specific story of forgiveness

This generous young man (and a close friend) was Rory, who has now graduated. The day that Rory had a chance encounter while handing out kids' tennis balls which escalated into much more. As he continued to walk around the city, he, amongst other things, met a homeless man, the brother of movie star, who was searching for his long-lost son (and Rory's contact with this man was in the paper Todd had with him later that fateful day). But in any event, the time Todd and the boys spent with Rory changed them. Gradually, their attitudes and behaviours at school began to change, and from his surprised family, Todd has blossomed. And the week-long visit over Easter vacation that year (in addition to the obligatory tennis balls, Rory had marched them to the top of the very many steps in sight of Todd's house) was filled with letters from the boys in Todd's class, three of whom were at Todd's house that entire week, or from their parents, thanking him. The most touching message was from Todd's teacher. His class had never written a 'thank you' letter before and, with all their emotional, family, and economic problems, normal school pressure had not allowed her to encourage them to do so until then.

They had had so many supply teachers that year, and she did not have time to write herself, but had read aloud the letter from Todd's mother, Kate, who told Rory what the visit and their new bond had meant to all of them. Kate wrote about her feelings of isolation (but how she would not be run out of the neighbourhood where her children had been born) and pressed her disbelief, exbut how 'proud and thrilled' she was to see her children inhaling books and rushing to school. Before handing out the presents from Rory, she asked the boy who was overly fidgeting to slow down and thanked Rory for 'helping those boys to change.' She reminded team Ruth that 'maybe their fathers had never shown them such attention.'

Lessons Learned

There are, then, a number of lessons I have learned about forgiveness from my survivors that continue to serve me well both personally and professionally. Religion and spirituality are far from the only sources of forgiveness, but certainly they have been one of the major vehicles of bringing this virtue to the world. Forgiveness is not a solo act and often takes the support and inspiration of others to be realised. Forgiveness often has steps to it, and sometimes the steps can take a long time. Part of the healing path after betrayal is acknowledging the wrong done, speaking the hurt aloud, requesting support, receiving and giving care, feeling the feelings that forgiveness requires, and of course learning the skills and identifying the intention to try forgiveness on. Finally, we are

not here to judge but rather to guide. Often people come up to me after my talks, doing what I call a "forgiveness confession," telling me about their troubled relationships, confiding in me, and then asking me what they should do. I politely pass on giving any hard and fast advice, usually responding with the following: "I cannot tell you that. But what has your heart been telling you about that very question?" The website is full of exercises that can help wonderer forgive, one of which is the Promise.

Reflecting on insights gained from personal forgiveness experiences

In my process of reflecting on how the experiences I have had with forgiveness have contributed to my knowledge about forgiveness and the impacts on my work, I have become aware of the personal impact that a journey to forgiveness has for the persons involved. Whether forgiveness is offered, requested or not, taking a deliberate step into a process that means confronting one's utmost feelings towards oneself, another, the experience that elicits the need for forgiveness, or the circumstances that create the conditions where forgiveness can flourish or remain in the realm of possibilities, engender profound reflection. It generates opening and closing of emotional and spiritual aspects that can have very significant impacts in the persons involved.

Research can present the process that a person can go through in order to arrive at a point where forgiveness, that is, the acceptance of the fact that it was its exercise or non-exercise that gave peace, restoring internal balance, or acceptance of the impossibility of forgiveness, and feeling peace in relation to the transgressor. However, personal and direct experience can enlarge this understanding by being illuminated by its very significance without the need of further anesthetising it.

Inspiring Others

In caring for crisis-affected children, I have learned that inspiration is setting an example, acting as a model for others. In an ideal world, those we meet could be lifted to new heights by our serenity, our success, our vision. But in the real world, one of the most common human failings is the instinct to feel demoralised by others' happiness or success. In such situations, inspiration is more effective than any other influence. For anyone wishing to help others, this is an enormous challenge - perhaps the biggest of all - to live in such a way that one's actions inspire others. Inspiration involves action, for we are not inspired by words but by deeds. It requires a pattern, a role model; someone who is living the examples of truth and abiding love. Although the phenomenon of inspiration cannot be scientifically measured, we can recognise inspiration when we see it. Inspiration doesn't necessarily involve great gestures or grand moments. Those people who find fault with others all too often believe that the only way to help those less fortunate is by doing something direct, grandiose or sensational. But the reverse is true. A spirit of humility and simple real-life examples can be far more effective than any other. Anyone who deals with people expects them to have inherent flaws and failings. It's informed by this knowledge that we can effectively teach others. Initially, we all learn through observation, through association and through assimilation, and I have found this especially true in my own attempts to deal with others.

Positive messages

"I hope I inspire people to keep moving forward" have realistic expectations about the process - be patient and allow yourself to grieve and heal. They also recommend that readers avoid being completely isolated and that it is important to maintain perspective and have balance and that it is neither necessary nor desirable to become completely selfless. You should establish healthy personal boundaries - to be fair with yourself and realise that this is "your" journey. Make a consistent effort to empower readers and demonstrate that healing is possible and discuss the possibilities of creating a more positive future. Express optimism that despite the challenges, you will "come out on the other side with a beautiful result."

About the Author:

Dr. Anjula Murmu, from Dumka, Jharkhand, India, is a renowned academician and social advocate. She authored the essay "Embracing Emotional Pain" in the book on Forgiveness by LOSD and serves as an Assistant Professor at Sido Kanhu Murmu University. With over 15 years of experience as a counsellor resolving domestic violence and couple disputes, Dr. Murmu has published two poetry collections and an anthology. She empowers tribal women through education and creative expression, earning numerous awards. Dr. Murmu is also an Independent Director at The Fertilizer and Chemicals Travancore Limited (FACT).

CHAPTER 5

Is FORGIVENESS a choice?

Dr. Renetta Weaver

Webster's dictionary defines forgiveness as "to cease to feel resentment against an offender" or "to give up resentment of or claim to requital." But in my journey, I've come to see forgiveness differently. To me, forgiveness is letting go of empty calories—those offenses that weigh us down emotionally without nourishing our souls. It's about releasing the emotional weight we carry, freeing ourselves from the burden of past hurts.

What's your definition of forgiveness? Take a moment to consider what it means to you. Is it a release? A fresh start? Or perhaps a gift you give yourself? Forgiveness, I've learned, is a choice. But here's something crucial to understand, not forgiving is also a choice. Both are personal decisions based on your definition of forgiveness and your values. When we choose to forgive, we open ourselves up to healing, growth, and newfound freedom. When we choose not to forgive, we remain tethered to our past, carrying the weight of resentment and pain with us wherever we go.

The science of unforgiveness is compelling and sobering. Research has shown that holding onto grudges and resentment can have severe impacts on our physical and mental health. Did you know that approximately two-thirds of all physical pain has an emotional root? And at the core of that emotional pain, we often find unforgiveness. When we don't forgive, our bodies remain in a state of stress. This chronic stress can lead to increased inflammation, weakened immune function, and a host of physical ailments. It's as if our bodies are carrying the literal weight of our emotional burdens. Moreover, unforgiveness can trap us in a cycle of negative emotions. It's linked to higher rates of depression, anxiety, and even post-traumatic stress disorder. The mental energy required to maintain grudges and resentment can leave us emotionally exhausted, hindering our ability to form and maintain healthy relationships.

But here's a challenging question to consider: If you can't forgive others, can you forgive yourself? Often, the hardest person to forgive is the one staring back at us in the mirror. Yet, self-forgiveness is crucial for our wellbeing and personal growth. Let's be honest: forgiveness is hard. It's not a magic wand that instantly erases hurt or makes everything okay. It requires courage, vulnerability, and often, a lot of inner work. But here's the thing: not forgiving is hard too. It's a different kind of hard—the kind that slowly eats away at your joy, your relationships, and your sense of self. So, I say: choose your hard. Choose the hard that leads to growth, to freedom, to a lighter heart. Choose the hard that opens up possibilities rather than closing them off.

But how do we do it? How do we forgive when every fibre of our being wants to hold onto the hurt, to protect ourselves from being wounded again? Let's break it down:

Who do we forgive?

Often, we think of forgiveness as something we offer others. And yes, that's a crucial part of it. We forgive those who have hurt us, intentionally or unintentionally. But there's someone else we need to forgive, someone we often overlook: ourselves. Self-forgiveness can be the hardest, yet most transformative act of all.

What do we forgive?

We forgive actions, words, and even thoughts that have caused us pain. We forgive broken promises, betrayals, and disappointments. But we also forgive ourselves for our mistakes, our perceived failings, and the times we didn't live up to our own expectations.

When do we forgive?

There's no perfect timing for forgiveness. It's not something that happens on a schedule. Sometimes, we're ready to forgive almost immediately. Other times, it takes years before we can even consider it. The important thing is to forgive when you're ready, not when others tell you should.

Where does forgiveness happen?

Forgiveness happens in our hearts and minds. It's an internal process, though it can certainly be aided by external factors like therapy, conversations with loved ones, or spiritual practices. The "where" of forgiveness is wherever you are when you make that choice to let go.

How do we forgive?

This is often the trickiest part. How do we actually go about forgiving? It starts with acknowledgment—recognising the hurt and its impact on your life. Then, it involves a conscious decision to let go of the resentment. This doesn't mean forgetting or excusing the offense, but rather choosing not to let it control your life anymore. It often involves empathy, trying to understand the other person's perspective (or your own, in cases of self-forgiveness). And finally, it requires practice. Forgiveness isn't a one-time event, but a process we may need to recommit to daily.

Why should we forgive?

We forgive for ourselves. Not for the person who hurt us, not because someone tells us we should, but because forgiveness frees us. It releases us from the prison of our past and allows us to move forward unburdened by old hurts. The science is clear: forgiveness can lead to improved mental health, better physical wellbeing, and more fulfilling relationships. My own journey with forgiveness began on a summer day

when I was ten years old. I was playing on my Sit and Spin in the driveway, laughing as the world whirled around me. It was just another day, or so I thought. But that was the day my world really spun around, in a way I never expected. My neighbour, someone I thought I could trust, told me to come have fun at his house. My brothers, who were supposed to be watching me, were off doing typical teenagethings, leaving me alone and vulnerable.

What happened next broke my world apart. In just a few minutes, my understanding of safety, trust, and even the meaning of "fun" changed forever. Fun turned to fear, and innocence was replaced by confusion and pain.

After it happened, he told me, "If you tell anyone, no one will believe you. And even if they do, they'll know it's your fault. "Those words became the foundation for the walls I built around myself for the next twenty years. They made me unable to forgive—my neighbour, the adults who should have protected me, my brothers who weren't there, and most of all, myself. I didn't become afraid of men, but I developed a distorted belief that my only value was in pleasing others, particularly men, with my body. This led to a pattern of people-pleasing that extended far beyond just my interactions with men. I started studying all the time. Getting perfect grades became another way to please others and prove my worth. It was my way of showing the world—and trying to convince myself—that I had value beyond my body.

But no matter how many A's I got or awards I won, I still felt broken inside. This terrible experience changed how I saw everything. Like the tornado in "The Wizard of Oz," it had picked me up and dropped me in a confusing new world. And like Dorothy, I was desperately trying to find my way back home—not to a place, but to a sense of self-worth and wholeness that didn't depend on pleasing others. For years, I walked through life wearing masks. There was my Work Mask: Dr. Renetta, the smart, caring, always-in-control clinical director. My Party Mask: all smiles and easy laughter, the perfect wife and host. My Friend Mask: the good listener who never asked for help herself. And the mask I wore with my husband: a perfectly happy wife.

These masks were exhausting. Always pretending, always performing, never allowing myself to just be me. The weight of unforgiveness was like walking with a pebble in my shoe. That little tiny thing that irritated me every time I tried to walk forward, that thing that affected every interaction, every decision. When my husband would try to hold my hand, I'd remember all the times I'd been hurt before. I'd pull away, leaving him confused and hurt.

At work, the pebble in my shoe made me constantly afraid of failing. Even though I looked successful on the outside, I always felt like a fake. When someone gave me a compliment, it felt hollow because I knew they weren't seeing the real me.

How could they, when I'd buried that person so deep under all my pretending?

The turning point in my journey came when I put on a Tiffany blue wig. It might sound silly, but that wig represented so much more than just a new hairstyle. It was the real me—not the woman trying to fit in, but the authentic, vibrant, sometimes quirky person I'd been hiding. Standing in front of the mirror, the vivid Tiffany blue framing my face, I saw a glimpse of the real Renetta for the first time in years. She was still there, underneath all the pretending, waiting to be found again. Putting on that wig was like rebelling against all the rules I'd set for myself. It caused a stir, yes, but more importantly, it made me feel seen— really seen— maybe for the first time since I was a kid. The next big step was a talk

with my husband. I looked him in the eye and said, "The woman you married wasn't the real me. This is the real me," as I stood there with my Tiffany blue wig. "I'm starting to love her, and I need you to love her too." It was scary to be so open, to show my true self to the person closest to me. But it also felt freeing.

As I started living more honestly, being heard and seen for who I really am, I began to notice changes. Not just in how I felt, but in my body too. I started to let go of emotional and physical weight. My thoughts were changing my mind and my life. The stress that used to make me feel sick was replaced by positive thoughts that made me feel free. I found myself smiling more, standing taller, and feeling more excited about life. At work, I started being more real, which led to better connections with my clients and coworkers. I wasn't afraid to share my own experiences anymore, which surprisingly made me a better leader and therapist.

This journey of forgiving myself and being more authentic changed how I led others. I realised that to lead others well, I had to lead myself first. As I learned to face my fears, be more real, and be kinder to myself, I became better at leading others. My leadership style changed from one based on control and trying to be perfect to one based on understanding, being real, and working together.

The decision to forgive—myself, my abuser, those who failed to protect me—wasn't easy. It was a balance, weighing the costs and benefits. When I didn't forgive, I was constantly pretending to be happy, smiling, people-pleasing. But it left me feeling empty, anxious, and depressed. I was living proof of the scientific findings about unforgiveness—my emotional pain was manifesting in physical symptoms, affecting every aspect of my life. When I chose forgiveness, I released not just emotional weight, but physical weight too. I became more authentic. My anxiety and depression improved. I found a happiness that wasn't based on others' approval, but on being true to myself. The process of forgiving others opened the door to forgiving myself, and that self-forgiveness was the key to my transformation.

Forgiveness isn't a one-time decision. It's a journey, a daily choice to let go of the past and embrace the present. Some days are easier than others. There are still moments when the old pain resurfaces, when I'm tempted to put the masks back on. But now I have tools to deal with these moments. I have my FORGIVE framework:

F - Face the Truth: Be brave and honest about your life.

O - Open Your Heart: Be kind to yourself and others.

R - Release the Past: Let go of old hurts that don't help you anymore.

G - Give Yourself Grace: Allow room for mistakes and growth.

I - Invest in Your Healing: Commit to making yourself better.

V - Validate Your Feelings: Recognise your emotions without letting them control you.

E - Embrace Your New Day: Move forward with hope and optimism.

This framework has become my guide, helping me navigate the tricky path of forgiving myself and being more real. It wasn't always easy, but with each step, I felt lighter, freer, more like myself.

Today, as I write this, I'm wearing my Tiffany blue wig. It's become a symbol of my journey, a reminder of the day I chose to be real instead of trying to fit in. The woman I see in the mirror now isn't perfect—she's wonderfully, gloriously imperfect. But she's real, she's whole, and she's free.

To those of you reading this who see yourselves in my story, I want you to know: it's never too late to start forgiving yourself. The power to change your life has been inside you all along. You just need the courage to take that first step. Remember, it's a new day. You have the power to rewrite your story, to choose forgiveness over holding grudges, being real over pretending. Follow the FORGIVE framework, tell your truth, and watch how your life changes. You'll find yourself not just happy, but really, truly happy, living a life that's true to you, free from the shadows of your past. The journey of forgiveness and finding yourself isn't always easy, but I promise you, it's worth it. Every step you take towards being real and forgiving yourself is a step towards a more fulfilling, joyful life. You deserve to live that life. You deserve to be free.

So, I'll leave you with this question: What mask are you wearing today, and are you ready to take it off? Remember, the choice to forgive—or not to forgive—is yours. But now that you understand the impact of that choice, which will you make?

The Book On Forgiveness

About the Author:

Dr. Renetta Weaver is a multifaceted professional, board certified in Metaphysics and licensed as a Clinical Social Worker. As a Neuroscience Coach, Certified Bariatric Counsellor, and Holistic Life Coach, she integrates diverse disciplines to enhance well-being. Dr. Weaver's expertise spans mental health, metaphysical practices, and holistic approaches, empowering clients to achieve comprehensive personal growth and wellness. Her commitment to transformative coaching and counselling reflects in her holistic approach, blending scientific knowledge with metaphysical principles to support individuals on their journey towards optimal health and fulfilment.

CHAPTER 6

Healing And

INSPIRATION

Jiaqi (Lucy) Yu

Webster's dictionary defines forgiveness as "to cease to feel resentment against an offender" or "to give up resentment of or claim to requital." But in my journey, I've come to see forgiveness differently. To me, forgiveness is letting go of empty calories—those offenses that weigh us down emotionally without nourishing our souls. It's about releasing the emotional weight we carry, freeing ourselves from the burden of past hurts.

What's your definition of forgiveness? Take a moment to consider what it means to you. Is it a release? A fresh start? Or perhaps a gift you give yourself? Forgiveness, I've learned, is a choice. But here's something crucial to understand, not forgiving is also a choice. Both are personal decisions based on your definition of forgiveness and your values. When we choose to forgive, we open ourselves up to healing, growth, and newfound freedom. When we choose not to forgive, we remain tethered to our past, carrying the weight of resentment and pain with us wherever we go.

The science of unforgiveness is compelling and sobering. Research has shown that holding onto grudges and resentment can have severe impacts on our physical and mental health. Did you know that approximately two-thirds of all physical pain has an emotional root? And at the core of that emotional pain, we often find unforgiveness. When we don't forgive, our bodies remain in a state of stress. This chronic stress can lead to increased inflammation, weakened immune function, and a host of physical ailments. It's as if our bodies are carrying the literal weight of our emotional burdens. Moreover, unforgiveness can trap us in a cycle of negative emotions. It's linked to higher rates of depression, anxiety, and even post-traumatic stress disorder. The mental energy required to maintain grudges and resentment can leave us emotionally exhausted, hindering our ability to form and maintain healthy relationships.

Meditating on "the power of forgiveness" has softened that chip on my shoulder. What about any other word than "forgiveness" would have brought me an assignment that ultimately plunged me into a meditation over the mouse that roared, the meek who shall inherit the earth – or make a good run at it at least? What other word would have fed me the meal from Jesus' Sermon on the Mount proclaiming the meek "blessed" and that had me dreaming up my own pivot-bottom story of regaining dignity while still respecting my humble soul?

Defining Forgiveness

It is difficult to imagine discussing forgiveness and the many reasons it is one of the most powerful actions anyone can perform without first defining what forgiveness truly is. To forgive, often mistaken as a sign of weakness, is not only challenging but difficult for most of us to perform. Quite the contrary, at its core is a strength that can lift enormous burdens from our spirit and ultimately lead us to healing; however, restoring a rapport with the offender is a whole other matter. Many times, that person might not wish for assistance, or may not desire to take an honest look at their behaviour and its consequences. And even with such conversations, expect no apologies or worse, be willing to undergo a series of further personal accusations and attacks. It is a strange paradox that lies at the heart of the healing forgiveness.

And it exists in a realm where party lines and countries, wars and personal attacks, religious, sexual and financial abuse are chronic issues. But forgiveness is nonetheless the gateway to healing. Moreover, there are two factors not part of the traditional definitions of forgiveness that are essential as we take our inner journey: experience and time. With those two, there's much that one can come to understand - at least theoretically. Although there are many people who feel comfortable with their definitions of forgiveness, over the years we have had people looking at us with questioning eyes when we share our own thoughts on this profound subject. And when this moment has transpired, they then replied, "I never thought of it in quite that way." Would you be willing to listen and learn what it is sitting "next to the indefinable"?

Significance of Forgiveness in Personal Growth

I suffered from the idea of having been badly wronged and victimised for many years. Then, I started to think that maybe it was through my very suffering that I accumulated so much strength. Though my struggles with others had originally been the cause of much pain and tears, it was because of these conflicts that I have come to know myself so well. And, once I recognised this, I knew that I had reached a magnificent harbour in the search for myself. Forgiving, releasing all instincts for vengeance, and ceasing the generations-long family cycle of hating and being hated allowed me to join the world of infinite and incorruptible wisdom for the first time in my life. Since that day, I have felt pride in the immense well of freedom, patience, tolerance, happiness, and peace I have created within myself. Now no one and nothing can phase me.

As the person who frees herself through self-liberation – that is, who achieves self-enlightenment – I believe that the power of forgiveness can break the shackles that bind it. The journey to personal forgiveness does not end in self-satisfaction; it is selfish to stop at self-forgiveness and denies oneself the other half of self-liberation. After arriving at a state of self-satisfaction, I then glorify the act of forgiveness. After liberating themselves, they forgive by serving as examples of self-liberation and thus helping others achieve it. Through the act of forgiveness, the freed person can free others; many people are waiting for that power.

The Book On Forgiveness

My Personal Experience

Forgiving and letting go of disillusionment can be most essential in allowing someone to continue living, gleaning a new awareness and understanding about life. When inconsiderate, hurtful, unkind, or negative remarks and actions are continually directed toward individuals, the damaging toxic accumulation of unresolved anger, hostility, and internalised pain lay the foundations of emotional and mental decline. It becomes necessary to replace the collective layers of bitterness hindering emotional and mental growth, with an open-minded acceptance before the accumulated layers become too hard to remove and replace.

I can only relate my personal experiences about the power of forgiveness and the significant impact it had on my existence. In the world we live, spiritual dysfunction creates scars and disintegration at the soul level. Can you imagine someone apologising to you, whether deserved or not, for unkind words or actions? Do all the sensations associated with negative processes including demonstration of a sense of implicitness, make it easier for forgiveness to enter your spiritual realm and can you accept the apology and truly mean it, remembering the hurt, the pain, the anguish? Dips in life's road encouraged the spiritual development for me, unfolding into an anchor where my spirit educates at a spiritual dimension. Entering the rapids of emotional instability or mental risk allow the snowball phenomenon to build against me; fortunately, I have embraced the sense of spiritual unity: the wholeness of word, thought, and respect.

Testing My Capacity for Forgiveness

More than a thousand days after witnessing the execution of my onlyGeneral andand his grandmother and her two friends, one kind member of the media asked me what went through my head when I sat down in the room in the University of Montana Law School where the leader of the law enforcement, Attorney General Mike McGrath, was explaining to me how the trigger was pulled, determining in unbelievable detail how the job was done in the relative dark of his home, hiring a famous coroner to pronounce over my son and his grandmother's four body parts, and looking me in the eye many hours later telling me that he had just acted as Attorney General, and offering me his condolences.

I spent the first few seconds desperately trying to keep the contents of my stomach in check. Then, I finally stood up and told him I believed in my God and I forgave the shooter, and that God would judge his actions. Then, I told him about me and the things I was glad of and mentioned the casket, which was a much more effective tool than my words.

Lessons Learned

My experiences have taught me valuable and important lessons. I believe these lessons are universal. It didn't take a miracle. It didn't take a life-threatening illness. And despite the many obstacles along the way, it didn't take all that long. It's part of my past, but I don't live there anymore. I can't change the painful past events. Trying to do so would only focus more energy on worthless pursuits. I can, however, take from these events and grow. I believe that I really can rise above the situation. I can learn from it and move on. From that moving on, I can create good things. Whether I can create a wonderful life is still very much up to me. That remains my most challenging quest. I believe that no matter who you are, what you've been through, forgiveness is a gift you can give yourself.

Yes, we'll still have good days and bad. There will be moments of self-doubt and setbacks. Sometimes the struggle will seem utterly overwhelming. But I believe it's worth it. The peace and joy, the lightness of spirit that follows in the wake of forgiveness, the smiles that can only be sincere, to know what lies behind them, are simply beyond description.

The Book On Forgiveness

My experiences have taught me valuable and important lessons. I believe these lessons are universal. It didn't take a miracle. It didn't take a life-threatening illness. And despite the many obstacles along the way, it didn't take all that long. It's part of my past, but I don't live there anymore. I can't change the painful past events. Trying to do so would only focus more energy on worthless pursuits. I can, however, take from these events and grow. I believe that I really can rise above the situation. I can learn from it and move on. From that moving on, I can create good things. Whether I can create a wonderful life is still very much up to me. That remains my most challenging quest. I believe that no matter who you are, what you've been through, forgiveness is a gift you can give yourself.

Empathy and Understanding

Hatred breeds more hatred and anger. We must have empathy and understanding for those who hate us, realising that they are not justified in their hatred. This can be a difficult if not impossible lesson to learn, especially if you were a victim of genocide or narrowly managed to escape death in war. However, if hatred becomes the governing emotion that rules our lives, then the enemy has won, for they have coarsened our humanity, diminished our souls, and broken our spirit. To me, the most important

loss for a victim is the high premium they place on revenge and the resulting concept that peace is simply a break between wars. I wish that neither war nor the loss of a loved one had been my teacher of the importance of forgiving and learning how to connect spiritually with others. There are many paths to forgiveness. In the realm of human rights, some paths are legal and others are traditional, some believe in seeking justice at the expense of forgiveness and others hold that forgiveness should take precedence over justice. As the Dalai Lama rightly confirms, "It is much more dignified to forgive without demanding that the person who wronged you ask for forgiveness." Because monster needed for flow to be complete. That is the tragedy of many Holocaust survivors.

Letting Go of Resentment

Letting go implies acceptance. And here's the beautifully paradoxical part: accepting things as they are leads to change, to being a responsible person in relation to these things and doing whatever we can to improve them. Similarly, accepting, understanding and loving ourselves as we are taking the first step to change our negative tendencies. But to accept is not to resign ourselves to the unjust pattern of life, or to the design of a society. In our personal lives, our society should be transformed through love, not by resentful condemnation. Whenever we are angry, as they would say, we have to look deeply into the causes of suffering; then we will be able to respond to injustice with clarity, understanding, and great love.

I believe all people want to remember love, to drink from the healing elixir of a deeply loving heart. The power of love is such that it can erase all memory of what brought relief to heal us and can bring us to an all-time high. The state of love can wash away all pain, all embarrassment, all loneliness, denial and separation from the universe. No longer drowning in its own unhappiness, the heart can blaze a purifying trail through the crossfire of emotions and set an example capable of leading us all to the green door of bliss. This condition remains possible if we live completely in the 'now'. It has to be moment-to-moment action, constantly directed against the simplest problems we encounter personally. But to put such love into action is very difficult. That is the great potential and the greatest challenge of individuals and humanity. I am always filled with great joy and energy to be able to follow this path. But even with my heartfelt dedication I am not perfect, and I don't think anybody is. However, despite the difficulties we encounter, we often gain enjoyment, love and happiness just by trying to be an expression of universal truth.

Sharing the Journey

As a follow-up, what happened was that something shifted inside me. I don't have a lot of insight into what actually happened, but I suddenly felt different. It seemed as if my injured places had healed over and left me intact again. Some people might call this "healing." No one was as surprised as I was. I finally realised that if I could stand at the side of the open grave of the worst thing I could ever have imagined and feel better, maybe a healing story (or at least an inspiring one) had emerged from my life. I also realised after time had passed that the hard, hard clamshell of bitterness and anger had quietly opened without my knowledge, and I had emerged as someone else going out into the world to teach something to others about being healed.

I told my colleagues a little bit about my life, and they were fascinated with the change in me – even though they knew none of the specifics. They said I seemed so much happier and less anxious. I began to share with them this idea of forgiveness. I told them I wasn't at all sure that it was the answer to everything, but if there was someone in their life they needed to forgive, they might want to consider it. It really seemed to make a difference in their lives.

A couple of times my friends told me that whatever I was doing was really making a difference.

Sharing Experiences

I believe most people can relate to and empathise with the core struggles surrounding the process of forgiveness. While the source of trauma in our own lives and in our communities may be vastly different, the outcome is the same in that these tragedies shatter the protective bubble around our sometimes overly idealistic world views. On the other hand, thousands all over the world at any given moment in time. It is the ability to connect with the other survivors that gives each survivor the comforting confirmation that someone else can understand, if only in a small way, what they are feeling.

The emotion of grief is doing the only thing it knows how to do, and that is to support and sustain our survival. The realisation that what once was a real, tangible, earthly thing now exists only as a seeming figment of a fading memory that will eventually be but another page in our life history book is more than a fellow survivor. It is something that can help the healing begin. People often share experiences that are close in nature, as it is human nature to want to be understood and connect with others over common experiences. We need to release the overwhelming emotion of grief that fills the vacuum of a life too suddenly made less whole. Individuals that share similar experiences help the grieving to move from merely surviving in a hostile environment back to feeling a connection with others within this environment. Gathering collectively to vocalise a personal struggle and having the potential to lift are feelings that are too powerful to be alone.

As a result of our journey in coming to understand forgiveness as multi-layered, person-directed, and limitless, we believe important implications exist for counsellors and their clients. Counselling and the promotion of forgiveness are not activities without other agendas. Client welfare is the primary objective in any helping encounter; however, if forgiveness is an identified goal within the counselling process, a few key areas are important considerations: the client and his or her beliefs, the client's readiness for change, and the therapeutic environment. In so doing, we are advocating a values-based rather than a value-informed therapy.

We value helping clients to live healthy, satisfying lives, but we are not assuming that our values are universally shared simply because they are inherent in our model of counselling.

Likewise, if client beliefs contribute to misery and disease, terminating counselling or implanting values is not an ethical stance. Such actions are incongruent with ethical guidelines and professional traditions of counselling. The values-based approach suggests that an encounter can only take the path that the client is willing to travel. Counsellors can participate as guides adept at helping clients navigate the journey of the counselling dynamic as each client reaches the desired destination of self-understanding and personal transformation. Our response to the experience of forgiveness encourages counsellors to consider a beginning place where forgiveness could become a service within their profession. The counselling arena can offer a setting for forgiveness by being the ultimate sanctuary in whose confines deeply troubling wounds can be soothed, psychological remnants disposed, and a return to relational health encouraged.

Inspiring to Embrace Forgiveness

There are events in our lives that are appropriate opportunities for us to bring the message of learning and practicing the gift of forgiveness to help inspire others. Perhaps the only thing worse than enduring the hurt caused by being wronged is to allow the negative power of animosity, bitterness, and continued anger to overtake our life. Unfortunately, many people become prisoners of that pain for a very long time. Sharing our own personal journey toward understanding and celebrating the healing power of 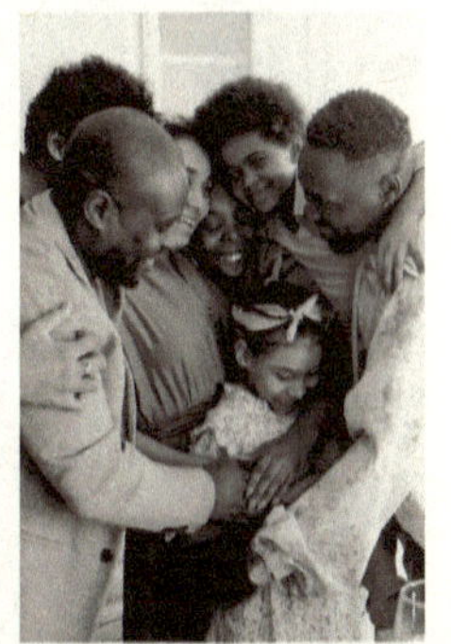 forgiveness may help someone presently going through a difficult time in their life begin to explore ways to working toward healing themselves, no matter what situation is causing their anger. Sharing the process of self-discovery and understanding of what it really means to offer the gift of forgiveness to those who have profoundly hurt us can enlighten and uplift a fellow traveller. The shared experiences might also challenge fellow companions to consider what they need to examine in their own lives to move toward healing.

The Book On Forgiveness

Our own life journey and learned experiences has also allowed us to become seasoned enough to recognise the thrill of extending true forgiveness, knowing we are no longer prisoners of the negative emotions previously generated by wrongs that had nestled for a long time in our hearts. Furthermore, we are able to recognise a person who has embraced and offers the power of forgiveness to a person or event that has caused pain and suffering, because they emit a peculiar glow in that they are unencumbered by heavy burdens no matter the depth of previous plight. Their presence extends a silent and calming invitation that draws grateful teams of fellow travellers eager to learn how to celebrate the same gift of personal freedom.

About the Author:

Jiaqi (Lucy) Yu serves as a consultant at Deram Limited, a privately held, full-service development, investment, immigration consulting, and management company operating in Europe and Mexico. With a focus on diverse developments, our portfolio showcases successful projects spanning various asset classes, achieved through robust partnerships. Over nearly two years, we have demonstrated adaptability and growth, emphasising our commitment to excellence in every venture. Jiaqi (Lucy) Yu's expertise contributes to our mission of delivering comprehensive solutions and fostering sustainable development, ensuring clients receive tailored strategies for success in both the European and Mexican markets.

CHAPTER 7

A Personal Journey of
HEALING JOURNEY
Dr. Tamika Ray-head

My world turned upside down on 25th April 2024. My ex-husband, James, had suffered a grand mal seizure and was fighting for his life in the ICU. As I rushed to the hospital, a whirlwind of emotions engulfed me - fear for James's life, concern for our daughter Victoria, and a rekindling of old resentments I thought I'd long buried.

The drive to the hospital was a blur of flashing lights and honking horns as I weaved through traffic, my heart pounding in my chest. I tried to focus on the road, but my mind kept drifting to James. Despite our tumultuous past, he was still Victoria's father, and the thought of losing him sent a chill down my spine.

When I arrived at the hospital, I found myself face to face with Deborah, James's current wife. The sight of Deborah brought a flood of bitter memories - the pain of James's infidelity, the shock of discovering their marriage had occurred before our own divorce was finalised. I felt my jaw clench and my fists ball up at my sides.

"What are you doing here?" I snapped, my voice sharp with barely contained anger.

Deborah looked taken aback. "I'm his wife," she replied, her own voice tinged with defensiveness. "I have every right to be here." The tension between us was palpable, threatening to overshadow the gravity of James's condition. It was only the arrival of James's godmother, Grace, that prevented the situation from escalating further.

Grace, a tall woman with kind eyes and a commanding presence, stepped between us. "Ladies," she said firmly, "this is not the time or place. James needs all of us right now."

I took a deep breath, trying to calm myself. I knew Grace was right, but the sight of Deborah made my blood boil. How could this woman, who had caused so much pain, stand there acting like she belonged?

The Book On Forgiveness

As the days turned into weeks, and weeks into months, James's condition remained critical. I found myself caught in a constant state of stress and anger. I battled with Deborah over medical decisions, argued with hospital staff about visitation rights, and struggled to support Victoria through the turmoil.

Victoria, at the age of 17, was caught in the middle of the adult drama swirling around her father's sickbed. I could see the toll it was taking on her - the dark circles under her eyes, the way her shoulders slumped when she thought no one was looking. But every time I tried to shield Victoria from the conflict, I found myself drawn back into arguments with Deborah.

One particularly heated exchange occurred over James's treatment plan. Deborah wanted to pursue an aggressive approach, while I, with my medical background, advocated for a more conservative route. "You're not his doctor," Deborah spat.

"You lost the right to make decisions for him when you divorced him." I felt my face flush with anger. "And you think you know what's best? You, who abandoned him when he was sick in Mississippi?"

The argument escalated until a nurse had to intervene, reminding us that we were in a hospital and our behaviour was disturbing other patients. As I stormed out of the room, I caught sight of Victoria's face - a mixture of embarrassment and disappointment that made my heart sink.

The situation reached a boiling point when evidence of Deborah's financial misconduct came to light. My initial reaction was one of vindictive satisfaction. "I knew it," I thought to myself. "I knew she couldn't be trusted." But as I watched Victoria's face crumple at the news, I felt a twinge of something unfamiliar. Was it guilt? Regret? I wasn't sure, but it made me pause and reconsider my reactions.

That night, as I sat alone in my kitchen, I found myself reflecting on the past few months. The constant anger, the bitter arguments, the stress that seemed to permeate every aspect of my life - was this really who I wanted to be? Was this the example I wanted to set for Victoria? It was during one of my late-night vigils by James's bedside that I had an epiphany. As I watched James's chest rise and fall with each breath, I realised that my anger wasn't helping anyone - not James, not Victoria, and certainly not myself.

In that quiet moment, with only the steady beep of the heart monitor for company, I decided. I couldn't continue like this. Something had to change, and that something was me.

This realisation marked the beginning of my journey towards forgiveness. It wasn't an easy path, nor was it a straight one. There were days when my resolve wavered, when a thoughtless comment from Deborah or a setback in James's condition would reignite my anger. But I persevered. I sought help from a therapist, Dr. Chen, who introduced me to techniques for managing my emotions and practicing empathy. At first, I was sceptical. How could I possibly empathise with Deborah after everything that had happened?

Dr. Chen gently guided me through exercises designed to help me see things from different perspectives. "Empathy doesn't mean you agree with someone's actions," Dr. Chen explained. "It's about trying to understand where they're coming from, even if you don't approve of what they've done." I also started journaling, pouring out years of pent-up hurt and resentment onto the pages. As I wrote, I began to see patterns in my own behaviour, recognising how my past pain was influencing my present actions. One journal entry stood out to me.

"I realised today that I'm not just angry at Deborah. I'm angry at James for betraying me, at myself for not seeing it coming, at the unfairness of life for putting us in this situation. But what good is this anger doing? It's not changing the past. It's not helping James's recovery. It's not making things easier for Victoria. It's just eating me up inside."

Slowly, almost imperceptibly at first, things began to change. I found myself able to sit in meetings with Deborah without my blood pressure skyrocketing.

I could discuss James's care with the medical team without my voice shaking with suppressed emotion.

One day, as I was helping James with his physical therapy exercises, he grasped my hand and looked at me with clear eyes. "I'm sorry," he said, his voice weak but sincere. "For everything."

In that moment, I realised that my journey of forgiveness wasn't just about Deborah. It was about forgiving James, and even about forgiving myself for holding onto my pain for so long. Tears welled up in my eyes as I squeezed James's hand. "I know," I said softly. "I'm sorry too."

This moment marked a turning point in my relationship with James. As his condition improved and he became more lucid, we were able to have conversations we should have had years ago. We talked about our failed marriage, about the hurt we had caused each other, and about our hopes for Victoria's future. My changing attitude didn't go unnoticed. Victoria, who had been walking on eggshells around both her parents, began to relax. One evening, as we sat together in the hospital cafeteria, Victoria turned to me with a small smile.

"Mum," she said, "I just wanted to say... I'm proud of you. I know this hasn't been easy, but you're handling it so much better now."

I felt a warmth spread through my chest at my daughter's words. I reached out and squeezed Victoria's hand. "I'm trying, sweetie. I'm really trying."

As James's condition improved and Victoria's high school graduation approached, I found myself reflecting on how far we'd all come. The anger that had once consumed me had been replaced by a sense of peace I hadn't thought possible. There were still challenges, of course. The legal battles over Deborah's financial misconduct were ongoing, and there were still disagreements over James's care. But I approached these issues with a newfound calmness and clarity.

One particularly pivotal moment came during a meeting with the hospital's legal team. Deborah, looking tired and defeated, admitted to her wrongdoing. "I was scared," she said, her voice barely above a whisper. "I thought if I didn't have control over the money, I'd lose everything. I know it was wrong, but I didn't know what else to do."

In the past, I would have felt triumphant at this admission. Now, I felt a surprising surge of compassion. I recognised the fear in Deborah's voice - it was the same fear I had felt when my marriage to James had fallen apart. "We'll figure this out," I found myself saying. "The important thing is that we're all here for James and for Victoria."

The look of surprise and gratitude on Deborah's face was something I would remember for a long time. On the morning of Victoria's graduation, my phone buzzed with a text from Deborah: "Congratulations to Victoria. I know I have no right to ask, but please tell her I'm proud of her." A year ago, this message would have infuriated me. Now, I felt a complex mix of emotions - sadness for what could have been, compassion for Deborah's pain, and gratitude for my own growth. After a moment's hesitation, I showed the message to Victoria. She read it; her expression unreadable. Then, to my surprise, Victoria nodded. "Thanks for showing me that, Mom," she said. "I'm glad you did."

As I helped James into his wheelchair and watched Victoria adjust her graduation cap, I felt a profound sense of peace wash over me. The journey of forgiveness had been long and often painful, but it had brought us to this moment - a moment of joy, pride, and hope for the future.

I knew that challenges lay ahead. James's recovery was ongoing, legal battles loomed, and family dynamics remained complex. But I faced these challenges with an open heart and a resilient spirit, knowing that forgiveness was not a destination but a continual choice - one I was ready to keep making, day after day, for myself and for my family.

As we made our way to the graduation ceremony, I squeezed James's shoulder and smiled at Victoria. In that moment, surrounded by the love of my family and the strength I'd found within myself, I felt a deep sense of gratitude for the healing power of forgiveness.

The auditorium was packed with proud families, the air buzzing with excitement. As Victoria's name was called and she walked across the stage to receive her diploma, I felt tears of joy spring to my eyes. I glanced at James, seeing my own pride reflected in his face.

After the ceremony, as we gathered for photos, I noticed Deborah hovering uncertainly at the edge of the crowd.

Taking a deep breath, I decided. I walked over to Deborah and, to everyone's surprise, including my own, I held out my hand.

After the ceremony, as we gathered for photos, I noticed Deborah hovering uncertainly at the edge of the crowd. Taking a deep breath, I decided. I walked over to Deborah and, to everyone's surprise, including my own, I held out my hand.

"Thank you for coming," I said. "I know it means a lot to Victoria."

Deborah took my hand, her eyes wide with surprise. "Thank you for letting me be here," she replied softly.

It wasn't a Hollywood ending. There were still hurt feelings, still issues to be resolved. But as I looked around at my unconventional family - my ex-husband, our daughter, his current wife - I realised that forgiveness had given us all a chance at a new beginning.

As we left the auditorium, stepping out into the bright sunshine of a new day, I felt a sense of lightness I hadn't experienced in years. The path of forgiveness had been difficult, but standing here now, I knew it had been worth every step.

My journey wasn't over. Forgiveness, I had learned, was a daily choice, a continual process of letting go and moving forward. But as I walked beside James's wheelchair, my hand on Victoria's shoulder, I felt ready for whatever lay ahead. I had found strength I never knew I possessed, and a capacity for love and forgiveness that had transformed not just my relationships, but my very self.

In that moment, under the clear blue sky of Victoria's graduation day, I felt truly free. Free from the burden of anger and resentment, free to love and be loved, free to face the future with hope and grace. And in that freedom, I found a peace I had never thought possible.

About the Author:

Dr. Tamika Ray- Head describes herself as nurturing, caring and creative. Born in the small rural town of Eastman, Georgia. She has a passion for God, her family and her community. She is the Founder of US-Based non-profit Pink STEM which has the Mission to provide a seat at the Head of the Table for Women in STEM Careers. Dr. Tamika Ray-Head was an "Air Force brat" raised primarily in Georgia, USA. She successfully went on to enjoy her career in the US. Air Force. During her tenure she was an Air Traffic Controller Supervisor and trainer (5 years), Administrative Assistant to the Company Commanders of the Operations Support Flight and the Medical Support Flight. Dr. Tamika Ray-Head's next journey began as an Educator where Her most recent teaching experience was as an Honors Science Teacher. She now owns and operates an after-school program "STEMuLate Your Mind Academy" focusing on tutoring students in Literacy and Complex Math Concepts to prepare them for STEM Careers. Her program is partnered with the DOD military base, Industry and local leaders. Tamika is married to her husband of the similar name Tamarco. With joy, they raise their blended family of six children.

CHAPTER 8

I'm Done Giving You Power Over My PAIN

Dr Demisha Burns

"My destiny is not behind me, so my focus won't stay there either." – DB

The weight of absence is a peculiar thing. It's not a tangible burden, yet it presses down on the soul with the force of a thousand unspoken words, a million unmade memories. For years, this absence shaped my world, a void where a father should have been. Let me set the record straight from the beginning that my Mother, although not perfect, did an amazing job as a single Mom and filled various roles along my journey; however, this story is not about her, it is about my Father and our journey, which was one that I didn't even expect and that would not have been possible, if forgiveness was not an option on the table.

Acknowledge

The first step was the hardest – acknowledging the pain that had become such a constant companion, it felt like a part of me. I had to face the truth: my father wasn't there.

Not for my first day of school, not for the moments when a little girl needed her dad to chase away the monsters under the bed, not even for the real monsters that would ultimately impact my life as well.
For so long, I treated him as if he were dead. It was easier that way, to mourn a ghost than to grapple with the living, breathing reality of his choice to be absent. But the pain didn't die with this pretence. It lived on, festering in the shadows of my heart.
I acknowledged the nights I cried myself to sleep, wondering what I had done wrong, the empty chair at my graduation that I had hoped he'd fill, along with the walk down the aisle that I desired to not take alone one day.

But acknowledgment isn't just about the pain. It's about honesty – with yourself and the world. I had to acknowledge that despite his absence, I had grown. I had become strong, resilient, and capable. I had to acknowledge that while he hadn't been there to protect me from the horrors I faced, I had survived. I had endured.

Be Aware of How It Makes You Feel

With acknowledgment came a flood of emotions – a torrent I had held back for so long, it threatened to drown me. Anger burned hot and fierce. How dare he abandon me? How dare he leave me vulnerable to the predators that lurked in the shadows of my childhood? Sadness washed over me in waves, mourning the relationship we never had, the memories we never made.

Betrayal stung sharp and bitter. I felt discarded, unwanted, like something easily forgotten. Shame crept in, whispering insidious lies – that I wasn't good enough, that I was unlovable, that I must have done something to deserve this abandonment. Fear, too, made itself known. Fear of trusting, even when I didn't understand why, of letting anyone close enough to hurt me again. Fear that I was somehow broken, damaged beyond repair by his absence and the traumas that followed.

But amid this storm of negative emotions, I found unexpected feelings too. Pride in my own strength and resilience. Hope that perhaps, one day, things could be different. And a tiny, fragile seed of love – not for the father he had been, but for the father he could potentially become.

Being aware of these feelings wasn't about wallowing in them. It was about understanding them, recognising their power and their source. It was about learning that emotions, even the painful ones, are teachers if we're willing to listen.

Choose to Change the Narrative

This is where the journey took an unexpected turn. I realised that while I couldn't change the past, I had the power to change the story I told myself about it. I could choose to remain the victim, forever defined by abandonment and trauma, or I could choose to change my narrative. I could tap into the love and support that was around me and press forward, continue to grow and excel despite the odds and be the one who found her strength in the struggle.

I chose to change the narrative. Instead of seeing myself as the girl left behind, I began to see myself as the woman who used her resources and the lack thereof to face her demons and emerge victorious. I chose to see my experiences not as things that broke me, but as forge fires that tempered my spirit.

This choice wasn't easy. It meant confronting hard truths about myself and my father. It meant challenging long-held beliefs and letting go of the comfort of familiar pain. But with each small choice to see things differently, I felt a shift within myself.

I chose to believe that my father's absence said more about his own struggles than my worth. I chose to see that while he hadn't protected me from harm when I was younger, I had been given the resources to learn to start protecting myself, while at the same time tapping into those supports that the Divine had already put in place behind the scenes. I chose to recognise that the love I craved from him was something that although not replaceable, was something that through my Mommy and support system could provide the base I needed to start healing and build upon.

Changing the narrative also meant allowing for the possibility of change in others. I had to open myself to the idea that people, including my father, could grow and evolve. That the man who I felt had abandoned me might not be the same man today and that there may have been more to the story about who he was and the experiences that had shaped his own narrative.

This choice to change my narrative was ongoing. Some days, it felt impossible. The old stories would creep back in, tempting me with their familiar pain. But each time I chose the new narrative, it grew stronger, more real.

Determine To Stop Giving Someone Power Over Your Pain

The final step was perhaps the most crucial – reclaiming my power. For years, I had given my father, and by extension, my pain, control over my life, even in his absence. My anger, my sadness, my fear – they dictated my choices, my relationships, my view of myself.

I determined that this would no longer be the case. I would no longer allow his absence to define my presence in the world. I would no longer let the pain of the past dictate the possibilities of my future.

This determination manifested in many ways. It meant setting boundaries – with myself and others. It meant learning to trust, even when it felt terrifying. It meant pursuing my dreams without the weight of "what if" holding me back.

I am determined to forgive – not for his sake, but for my own. Forgiveness didn't mean forgetting or excusing. It meant freeing myself from the burden of resentment. As often heard, it meant choosing to no longer drink the poison of bitterness, expecting it to hurt someone else.

This determination extended to other areas of my life as well. I faced the trauma of my past head-on, refusing to let my abusers hold any more power over me. I sought help, talked through my pain, and learned tools to manage the echoes of trauma that sometimes still reverberated through my life.

I am determined to love myself fiercely, to stop getting stuck looking for and blaming that other parent that I needed when I was young. I showered myself with the affection, the encouragement, the protection I had craved as a child. I tapped into my Higher Power as my safe haven and became open to receive and utilise the resources around me, acknowledging that I wasn't alone and didn't have to do things by myself.

As I reclaimed my power, something unexpected happened. The void that had been my father's absence began to fill – not with him, but with my Higher Power, my Mother's love and the love around me in unexpected spaces, including my godfather's who then helped me tap into my own worth, strength and love, my own sense of self.

And then, one day, when I was no longer looking for it, when I no longer needed it to feel whole – reconciliation became possible.

It started small – a phone call, tentative and awkward. Words stumbling over years of silence. But it was a start. As I listened to his voice, I realised that the man on the other end of the line was not the towering figure of my childhood fears and fantasies. He was just a man – human, flawed, not perfect like none of us are, struggling with his own demons, carrying his own regrets.

Our relationship grew slowly, cautiously. There were setbacks, moments when old pain flared and threatened to undo all the progress. But I held firm to my determination. I refused to let the past dictate our future.

The first time we hung out with no agenda, I felt a flutter in my chest – not of the desperate longing of my youth, but of a cautious, mature hope.

He showed me his birthplace, where some of the family I hadn't met stayed and talked about various experiences that we both had, including our joy of old schools, his new hobby of hunting, my hobby and passion of the range, in addition to some previous trauma in both of our lives and more. For the first time I felt like a little girl with my Daddy, safe, loved and protected. It was a gift I never expected to receive, made all the more precious by the journey it took to get there. And although I didn't know how long it would last, it felt amazing, and I wasn't going to fight it.

Father's Day came, for years, it had been a day of pain, of pointed reminders of what I lacked. But this year was different. This year, I spent it with him. We went to lunch and both talked at times and both were silent at times, but the silence between us was no longer painful. It was comfortable, filled with the promise of words yet to be spoken, of a relationship still unfolding.

This story of forgiveness and reconciliation isn't a fairy tale. It didn't erase the years of pain, the trauma I endured in his absence. It didn't undo the harm caused by those who took advantage of a vulnerable, fatherless child. But it opened a door I thought had been permanently closed.

Through this journey, I learned that forgiveness isn't a single act, but an ongoing choice. It's not about forgetting the past, but about choosing not to let it control your future. It's about reclaiming your power, your right to write your own story.

I learned that healing isn't linear. There are still days when the old pain resurfaces, when the weight of the past feels overwhelming. But now, I have the tools to face these moments. I know how to acknowledge the pain without letting it consume me. I understand my feelings and can sit with them without judgment. I can choose, again and again, to change the narrative. And I can determine, with each new day, not to let anyone else have power over my pain.

My relationship with my father is still a work in progress. We're learning, slowly, how to be in each other's lives. There's still hurt, still mistrust, still moments of awkwardness. But there's also hope, and growth, and the possibility of something we both thought was lost forever.

This journey of forgiveness hasn't just healed my relationship with my father. It's healed me. It's allowed me to forge healthier relationships, to pursue my dreams without the weight of the past holding me back. It's given me the strength to face other traumas, to extend forgiveness to others who hurt me – including, hardest of all, myself.

I've learned that forgiveness doesn't mean excusing the inexcusable. It doesn't mean allowing harmful people back into your life without change or consequences. Sometimes, forgiveness happens from a distance. Sometimes, it's a gift you give yourself, whether the other person deserves it or not.

In forgiving my father, I also found the strength to forgive my abuser. Not to excuse their actions, never that. But to free myself from the power their actions held over me. To recognise that their choices reflected their brokenness, not my worth. To understand that by holding onto hatred and blame, I was allowing them to continue hurting me long after the physical, sexual and verbal acts had ended.

Forgiving myself was perhaps the hardest part of all. Forgiving the little girl who blamed herself for her father's absence and for the abuse she endured by others.

Forgiving the young woman who made mistakes, who sometimes chose poorly in her desperate search for love and validation. Forgiving the part of me that still sometimes whispers that I'm not enough, that I don't deserve love or success.

But with each act of forgiveness, I reclaimed a piece of myself. I shed layers of pain, of self-doubt, of limitation.

I discovered strength I never knew I had, compassion I never thought I could feel, love I never believed I deserved.

This journey of forgiveness taught me that while we can't change the past, we have immense power over how it shapes our present and our future. We can acknowledge our pain without being defined by it. We can be aware of our feelings without being controlled by them. We can choose to change the stories we tell ourselves. And we can determine, every single day, to reclaim our power from those who hurt us.

Forgiveness, I've learned, isn't weakness. It's not letting someone off the hook or pretending the hurt never happened. It's an act of immense courage and self-love. It's choosing freedom over the false safety of familiar pain. It's opening yourself to the possibility of joy, of love, of a future unlimited by the chains of the past.

As I sit here, reflecting on this journey, I feel a sense of peace I once thought impossible. The little girl inside me, so long neglected and afraid, finally feels seen, feels loved, feels safe. And it's not because I opened my heart to reconciliation with my father, or because I decided that my abuser was no longer going to have power over my pain, or because the past magically untangled itself.

It's because I chose to see ME, to love ME, to keep ME safe. It's because I acknowledged MY pain, felt MY feelings, changed MY story, MY narrative and reclaimed MY power. It's because I forgave – others, yes, but most importantly, I forgave MYSELF.

And in that forgiveness, I found freedom. Freedom to love, to trust, to hope, to dream. Freedom to change my narrative and write a new story – not as a victim, not as a survivor, but as the SHERO of my own tale. A tale of resilience, of growth and of the transformative power of forgiveness.

There is a saying that I created that holds true to this day which states, "My destiny is not behind me, so my focus won't be there either." This is not the end of MY story. It's a new beginning, full of possibilities. And whatever comes next, I face it with an open heart, secure in the knowledge that I have the strength to overcome, the wisdom to grow, and the power to forgive – again and again and again. HOW ABOUT YOU?

About the Author:

Dr. Demisha Burns, also known as Dr. D, Mama D, and Kamali, is a renowned social work leader with a Doctorate in Social Work from Clark Atlanta University. With over 20 years of experience, she champions diversity, equity, inclusion, and belonging (DEIB), focusing on sexual and women's health, HIV/AIDS, STIs, and mental health. As a survivor of domestic violence and sexual abuse, Dr. Burns empowers marginalised individuals, groups and organisation through her businesses, Makn' Movz' and Sis Unleashed. Her mantra, "STOP TRYING TO FIT INTO A MOLD THAT YOU WERE MEANT TO CREATE!" reflects her advocacy for authenticity and self-determination.

CHAPTER 9

The journey to
SELF FORGIVENESS:
A Story Of Growth And Grace
Felicia Muhammad

In the projects of a bustling city, a young girl named Felicia began a journey that would teach her the true meaning of forgiveness. Raised by a hardworking single mother and influenced by her absent father, Felicia's path was shaped by her experiences in church, school, and the complicated world of adolescence.

1. **Felicia:** Our protagonist, an introspective, shy only child and is an 'ole soul' who is a mature, shapely teenager

2. **Felicia's mother:** A hardworking single parent

3. **Felicia's father:** An over-the-road truck driver with many children

4. **The older boy:** Felicia's first sexual partner

5. **The boyfriend who cheated:** A significant relationship in Felicia's community   college years

6. **Felicia's childhood friend:** The woman involved in the boyfriend's infidelity

Every Sunday, young Felicia would wake to an empty house, her mother already at work. She was considered at this time a Latch-key child. She'd prepare for church, sometimes catching the bus at her house, other times walking to Newton Center to board with other church goers from the projects. These Sundays, filled with scripture and song, laid the foundation for Felicia's complex relationship with faith and forgiveness.

As an only child, Felicia was introspective and shy, yet her physical appearance often drew unwanted attention. In elementary school, she was teased for her full lips, with cruel classmates accusing her of sexual acts she barely understood. This early exposure to sexuality and shame would follow her into adolescence, shaping her self-image and relationships.

Felicia's father, though not married to her mother, played a significant role in her life. As an over-the-road truck driver, he would take Felicia on summer trips across the country. Felicia adored him, seeing him through rose-coloured glasses despite his flaws. It wasn't until later that Felicia realised how his absences and relationships with multiple women had affected her own approach to love and attention.

The pivotal moment of Felicia's young life came on a hot summer day when she lost her virginity to a boy four years her senior. The experience was a mix of pain and pleasure, leaving Felicia feeling conflicted and ashamed. "I remember thinking, oh Lord, I am a sinner and going to hell. I was so scared," Felicia recalls. This event coincided with the loss of her grandmother, compounding her emotional turmoil.

As Felicia moved into middle school and high school, she found herself drawn to older men, recognising later that this attraction stemmed from seeking the attention she felt she didn't receive from her father. Despite her inner struggles, Felicia excelled socially, forming girl performance groups and participating in talent shows. It was during this time that a male friend revealed to Felicia that many boys found her intimidating due to her maturity, a revelation that both relieved and confused her.

Looking back on her journey, Felicia recognised the power of self-forgiveness. "It wasn't until years later that I finally forgave myself," she reflects. This realisation came after years of grappling with her experiences, her faith, and her self-worth.

Felicia's relationship with God evolved over time, becoming more personal and conversational. "As I read scriptures and talked to God like He is my best friend, I knew the truth, and that was all that mattered," Felicia shares. This deepening faith helped her navigate the challenges of high school and beyond.

1. The Sunday morning routine: Young Felicia, alone in the projects, preparing for church, symbolising her early independence and faith.

2. The summer road trips with her father: Felicia sitting high in the truck cab, watching the country roll by, unaware of the complex emotions these trips would later evoke.

3. The talent show performances: Felicia and her friends, dressed in matching outfits, singing New Edition songs, showcasing her resilience and joy in the face of inner turmoil.

4. The moment of betrayal: Felicia walking in on her boyfriend and childhood friend, the shock and pain etched on her face, marking a turning point in her understanding

Felicia's journey to forgiveness required her to confront her own actions and choices. She had to acknowledge her role in seeking attention from older men and recognise the patterns stemming from her relationship with her father.

"Due to all of my experiences, many spared from this publication, it was later revealed to me that I needed to forgive myself first," Felicia explains. This realisation marked a significant turning point in her life. Felicia, allowing her to extend forgiveness to others more easily.

Felicia's journey of forgiveness yielded several profound lessons:

1. Self-forgiveness is the foundation for forgiving others.

2. Faith can be a source of strength and guidance, even when questioning it.

3. Early experiences shape us but don't define us.

4. Maturity and self-awareness are crucial in breaking negative patterns.

5. Forgiveness is an ongoing process, not a one-time event.

6. Sharing one's story can be a powerful tool for healing and helping others.

"I am currently empowering others to know how to have the courage, self-trust and self-love to forgive yourself first," Felicia concludes. "This makes it so much easier to forgive others."

Felicia's story serves as a testament to the power of self-reflection, faith, and forgiveness. Her journey from a shy girl in the projects to a woman capable of forgiving deeply personal betrayals illustrates the transformative nature of self-forgiveness. By sharing her experiences, Felicia offers concrete guidance to old and new generations grappling with similar challenges, proving that it's possible to overcome past hurts and find peace through forgiveness.

About the Author:

Felicia Muhammad, a pioneering force in totalistic transformation, shatters limiting beliefs and ignites dormant potential through her groundbreaking S.elf H.ealing I.nner T.alk (S.H.I.T.) Shifting Subconscious Reprogramming journey. As a dynamic cornerstone of Oneness Wellness Lifestyles, she purposefully partners with Shifa Ali-Scott to disrupt conventional holistic wellness paradigms, offering Totalistic cutting-edge healing services, and toxin-free skincare to soul care. For over three decades, Felicia's magnetic presence and uncompromising dedication to purposeful living sparks profound awakenings, propelling countless individuals to reclaim their health, wealth, and personal power authentically.

CHAPTER 10

Recognising the unseen chains of

FORGIVENESS

Sharontine Bottley

Forgiveness and The Process of Forgiveness

The process of forgiveness was a long-awaited journey for me partially because I didn't know that it needed to be released. Because of this hidden task, I was delayed in recognising my purpose in life. Because I didn't recognise that forgiveness was a missing component to my progress in life, I was not able to start the process of defining who I was and figuring out what I was to do with this life that I had been handed. There were so many pivotal moments in my life that I know should have been the green light for me to move to the next level, yet it took me so much longer to recognise that I needed to forgive. It's so amazing to look back now and to reflect on just how important it was for me to learn how to forgive myself as well as others. If I hadn't grasped this concept, then it would have taken me further off the beaten path of acknowledging and recognising who I was and how I was supposed to navigate through this thing called life. I had to come face to face with the questions of how and why it took me so long to realise that there were places on my horizon that required my forgiveness before I could go on in life accordingly. This required that I forgive myself "first". So many times, life presents it the opposite way, but it never works. You can't start a successful path in life with the wrong ingredients. Forgiveness is often better served with Love.

The Book On Forgiveness

94

Unforgiveness Is a Silent Burden

The thought of carrying a small thing for a long period of time is exhausting let alone mentally and emotionally taxing. I never knew that the correlation between unforgiveness in certain areas of my life was weighing so heavily on me physically, mentally, and emotionally. Sometimes life's delivery is not always as we expect, and we have to work backwards to figure out why things aren't adding up or yielding the results that we think that we should be receiving. Oh, how I wish that it were easy enough to detail but it's not. Oftentimes, we have to fail over and over at something before we can get the results that we are expecting. Example: A person who lacks forgiveness and love may not see the direction of their life path as easily and as clearly as the person who's not bogged down with unforgiveness. It doesn't take a rocket scientist to figure out why. Yet, we spend an enormous amount of our valuable lifetime wondering what component(s) are missing. It's still very hard to believe that we can miss out on so many opportunities because of our traditional thinking and habits that limit us in so many areas. I have personally missed out on valuable opportunities because I had never healed in the area of forgiveness. However, one day my intuition kicked in and reminded me that I must forgive myself before I can truly and authentically forgive someone else. Here is when I realised that I was the reason for some of life setbacks. We all owe it to ourselves to do some praying and soul searching to release those things that hold us back. It all starts with forgiveness.

The Book On Forgiveness

The harbouring and nurturing of unhealed emotions and trauma such as unforgiveness can hold us back from achieving our life's greatest potential.

If we are going through life and we never reach our plateau, visions, and aspirations, then at some point, we ask ourselves why or what are we doing wrong that is hindering us from reaching our desired goals. By deep diving into my personal life stories and insights, it was revealed that I was one of low self -esteem which is why I was so quiet as I was growing up, I never voiced my opinion about certain things because I somehow believed that my opinion never mattered. Because I felt this way, I felt like others viewed me the same way. Nothing was further from the truth. I realised that I was the one initiating this thought and not others. So, I had to forgive myself for years of self-sabotage and unnecessary patterns caused by no one other than myself. They are the results of unaddressed pain, unspoken grievances, and unhealed emotional wounds that linger long after the events that caused them to have passed.

As these unseen chains became apparent in my life, I became keener on just how unrecognisable old wounds could manipulate your thought process, causing lingering resentment from past betrayals that affected my ability to trust others, both in personal relationships and professional settings.

The weight of carrying this emotional unrest would also impact my self-esteem and decision-making processes, often leading to missed opportunities. As I share these personal stories, I called these invisible barriers that were encountered as I stood firm in pursuit of my divine destiny. Because we were never taught what each season of life would look like, some of us may carry them for a lifetime and never really evolve. Again, as I will reflect on the moments that I recognised these unseen chains and the journey that I undertook to break free of them. This process involved deep introspection, confronting painful memories, and most importantly learning to forgive both myself and others.

Again, I share these poignant details as a reminder that true freedom comes from within and that letting go of the past is essential to moving forward and embracing a brighter future. My hope is that you'll walk away with an understanding of the importance of identifying and addressing your own unseen chains. You'll understand how acknowledging and working through past pain is a crucial step towards healing and personal growth.

Breaking Point

The day of reckoning was a pivotal moment for me, and I shall forever be reminded when the weight of unforgiveness became unbearable. In the depths of my darkest moments, It felt as though I was on the edge of a cliff between hope and despair. The weight of unforgiveness pressed heavily on my soul, a burden that seemed impossible to shed. I had faced countless trials, each one chipping away at my spirit, leaving me feeling shattered and lost. The pain of betrayal, the sting of harsh words, and the scars of past wounds all hit me like a heavy cloud. I found myself taking a step back to reassess everything as the weight of it all was too crippling.

Forgiveness, I learned, is not a one-time act. It is a process, a continuous journey of releasing and renewing. Through this journey, I discovered a profound truth: forgiveness is not a sign of weakness, but of immense strength. It takes courage to let go of the pain, to rise above the hurt, and to choose love and compassion over anger and resentment. Forgiveness does not erase the past, but it transforms our relationship with it. It allows us to reclaim our power, to write a new narrative for our lives—one that is not defined by our wounds, but by our capacity to heal.

As I continue on this path, I am reminded daily of the transformative power of forgiveness. It is a gift we give to ourselves, a bridge that leads us from pain to peace, from brokenness to wholeness. In forgiving, we create space for healing, for growth, and for the boundless possibilities that lie ahead.

So, I invite you to take this journey with me. To confront your own pain, to acknowledge the wounds that have held you captive. And in that acknowledgment, to find the courage to forgive. It will not be easy, and there will be days when the weight feels too heavy to bear. But remember, in every step towards forgiveness, you are reclaiming your power, your peace, and your purpose. Let us walk this path together, with hearts open to the healing that forgiveness brings.

The Power of Letting Go

There comes a time in each of our journeys when we must face the shadows that linger within us, a moment when we stand at the crossroads of holding on and letting go. It is a time of reckoning, where we must confront the negativity and pain that have taken residence in our hearts. For me, this journey was both daunting and transformative, a path that required me to acknowledge my own role in carrying the burdens that weighed me down. This practice of letting go became a form of self-care, a way of nurturing my soul and honouring my journey.

To anyone walking this path, I offer this: Embrace your pain, acknowledge your ownership, and then release it with compassion. Allow yourself to be guided by the wisdom of those who came before us, and trust in the goodness that awaits on the other side of letting go. It is a journey that leads to a life filled with light, love, and endless possibilities.

In letting go, we find our true selves. We reclaim our power, our peace, and our purpose. Let us continue this journey, carrying forward the torch of resilience and hope. Let us walk in the light of our liberation, free from the shadows of the past, and open to the boundless goodness of the present.

Forgiving Yourself

Growing up, we were always taught to forgive others and to extend grace, but rarely did we hear about the importance of forgiving ourselves. There was no map to navigate this crucial aspect of healing. The focus was always outward, never inward. Yet, as I walked through my own journey, I came to understand that self-forgiveness is not just a luxury; it is a necessity.

Self-forgiveness is an act of reclaiming our humanity. It is about recognising our own worth, despite our mistakes and shortcomings. In the eyes of our ancestors, who endured hardships and struggles beyond our imagination, self-forgiveness would have been an act of survival, a testament to their resilience. It is with their strength and wisdom that we can find the courage to forgive ourselves.

Once we have acknowledged our mistakes, the next step is to extend compassion to ourselves. Just as we would offer understanding and forgiveness to a loved one, we must offer it to ourselves. This means recognising that we are human, that we are bound to err. It means speaking to ourselves with kindness, rather than harsh criticism. I soon found out that in order to move forward, we must first heal our own wounds.

As we journey towards self-forgiveness, we must remember that it is not a one-time event, but a continuous process. In forgiving ourselves, we open the door to healing and growth. We create space for new opportunities, for joy, and for peace.

To all who walk this path, I say this: You are worthy of forgiveness. You are deserving of compassion and understanding. Take the time to acknowledge your mistakes, to feel their weight, and then let them go. Extend the same kindness to yourself that you would to others. Make amends where you can and commit to doing better. Remember that self-forgiveness is a journey, one that requires patience and persistence.

Let us walk it with the strength and wisdom of those who came before us, knowing that we are worthy of forgiveness and love.

Forgiveness Led to My Release / My Freedom

Freedom is a word that carries the weight of history, the dreams of our ancestors, and the promise of a brighter tomorrow. For me, the journey to forgiveness has led to this place of profound liberation, a release from the burdens that have long been woven into the fabric of my life. The power of forgiveness has set me free, and I stand here today, a testament to the strength and resilience of my lineage.

As I reflect on my path, I am filled with a deep sense of gratitude for the generations that came before me. Each thread in the tapestry of our family history holds a story of struggle and triumph, of pain and perseverance. Our ancestors endured unimaginable hardships, yet they pressed on, driven by a hope that one day, their descendants would know a life of freedom. It is to them that I owe a debt of gratitude, for their sacrifices have paved the way for my own journey of healing.

In learning to forgive, I have come to understand the importance of knowing the unknown. I delved into the depths of my own heart, uncovering the hidden wounds and unspoken pains that had shaped my beliefs and actions. I faced the darkness within, armed with the wisdom and strength of those who came before me. It was a journey of self-discovery, of peeling back the layers of hurt to find the light within.

Forgiving the unforgiven was no small feat. It meant letting go of the hurt and pain and choosing instead to embrace compassion and understanding. This act of forgiveness was not just for others, but for me as well. I learned to forgive the person I saw in the mirror, to release the guilt and shame that had weighed me down.

With each act of forgiveness, I felt the heavy burdens begin to lift. The chains that had bound me to my past were broken, one by one, and I was able to step into the light of a new day. This freedom was not just a physical release, but a spiritual and emotional liberation. I felt my spirit soar, no longer bothered by the weight of past hurts. I discovered a sense of peace and joy that I had long thought unattainable.

Freedom, I realised, is not just the absence of oppression, but the presence of possibility. It is the ability to dream, to hope, and to create a future that is not defined by our past. It is the power to shape our own destiny, guided by the lessons we have learned and the strength we have gained. In this state of freedom, I found a renewed sense of purpose, a desire to share my journey and to help others find their own path to purpose.

The journey to freedom is a testament to the power of forgiveness. It is a reminder that we have the ability to break the cycles of pain and suffering that has been passed down through generations. By choosing to forgive, we honour the struggles of our ancestors and pave the way for a future filled with hope and possibility.

As I conclude this chapter of my life, I do so with a heart full of gratitude and a spirit that is free. I carry with me the lessons of the past, the strength of my lineage, and the promise of a brighter tomorrow. I stand as a beacon of hope, a testament to the transformative power of forgiveness.

To anyone who reads these words, I offer this: May you find the courage to forgive, the strength to release your burdens, and the freedom to live your life fully. May you honour the legacy of those who came before you and create a future that is filled with light and possibility. This is the power of forgiveness. This is the gift of freedom.

About the Author:

Sharontine Bottley's background is in Finance and Economics. She endured several spiraling events including a tumultuous divorce, homelessness, depleted retirement and through it all, she never gave up. Her vision was and remains to help women that have been through unsurmountable pain and yet were left feeling a void and stuck by their circumstances. Ms. Bottley's purpose is to help them to move past their pain and find their purpose.

CHAPTER 11

LETTING THE RESENTMENT GO

Dr Anupma Bhardwaj

Lord Buddha once spoke about forgiveness, emphasising the ever-changing nature of individuals. He compared a person to a flowing river, never the same from one moment to the next. Similarly, when we forgive, we are not forgiving the same person who wronged us; both they and we have changed. This leads to a profound question: can we forgive immediately, or does forgiveness come with growth and experience?

My story of forgiveness began when I was pregnant with my first child. Pregnancy is a significant milestone, filled with dreams of holding a tiny baby, feeling their little hands, and seeing their cute smiles. The instinct of motherhood is so powerful that it seems our bodies are preparing for it from birth.

When I learned I was going to be a mother, my heart overflowed with joy, tempered with apprehensions. Questions flooded my mind: "Will I be able to take care of the baby properly?" "What if I unintentionally hurt the baby?" "Do I know enough about raising a child?" Despite these worries, the excitement of motherhood was overwhelming. The joy of knowing a tiny life is growing inside you is indescribable, but it also brings countless concerns.

During pregnancy, I was concerned about my low weight and whether I could provide enough nutrition for my baby. Adding to my anxiety, my husband, a police officer, was posted in a remote area. While the surroundings were serene, with greenery and fresh air, the lack of medical facilities was a constant worry. The unpredictability of police  work added to my stress. My husband could be called away at any moment, even in the middle of the night, leaving me anxious and unable to sleep. Hearing about accidents or kidnappings on the news deeply affected me, making me worry about the safety of my own child.

Eventually, we decided it was best for me to stay with my parents, given my anxiety and health concerns. Returning to my childhood home brought comfort and reassurance. My mother, a housewife and renowned writer, was ready to take care of me. The familiar environment and my parents' presence eased my mind.

However, my journey took a turn when I had to choose a gynaecologist. My mother's long-time doctor was experienced but strict, which frightened me. I chose a new doctor who was kind and gentle, but this decision led to unforeseen consequences.

At seven months pregnant, my doctor advised me to monitor the baby's movements closely. One day, I noticed reduced movement and immediately contacted her. She recommended an ultrasound, which revealed that the umbilical cord was wrapped around my baby's neck. This news shattered my peace, and I was admitted to the nursing home for observation.

The next day, my condition was deemed an emergency, and I underwent a C-section without my parents present. My son was born premature and underweight, with tubes attached to him for glucose. Seeing him in such a fragile state filled me with guilt and worry. The sight of my tiny baby under harsh phototherapy lights, struggling and uncomfortable, broke my heart. His skin turned brown from the ultraviolet lights, adding to my distress.

Over time, my son developed health issues, including food allergies. These challenges made me question my decisions and the doctor's competence, fostering resentment towards her. This guilt strained my relationship with my son, as I felt responsible for his condition. I blamed myself for not choosing a more experienced doctor, for not seeking a second opinion, and for not knowing enough about pregnancy and childbirth.

A turning point came when my husband was transferred to Haridwar, a spiritual place for Hindus. The sacred Ganges River, with its tranquil flow, brought a sense of peace. During an evening aarti by the Ganges, I listened to a saint speak about forgiveness and letting go of past grievances. This moment of spiritual clarity helped me realise that holding onto resentment was harming me more than anyone else.

I decided to forgive the doctor, accepting that everything happened as it was meant to. Writing a letter to her, expressing my forgiveness, brought me a sense of peace and improved my relationship with my son. Letting go of my anger and guilt allowed me to embrace the present and cherish my bond with my child.

Reflecting on this journey, I see how much I have grown. The experience taught me that forgiveness is not just about letting go of anger but also about embracing change and recognising our own growth. The person who hurt us is no longer the same, and neither are we. This realisation is liberating, allowing us to move forward without the burden of past grievances.

In conclusion, forgiveness is a journey that often requires growth and time. It is about recognising that both we and those who wronged us have changed. My story of forgiveness taught me that letting go of resentment can lead to inner peace and improved relationships. By forgiving, we allow ourselves to heal and grow, becoming

better versions of ourselves. This journey of forgiveness has made me more compassionate, understanding, and at peace with my past.

About the Author:

Dr Anupma Bhardwaj is a social worker of repute, with degree in law and doctorate in anthropology, worked extensively in the field of syncretinism and published paper on the same. She is a trained kathak dancer, and plays Vichitra Veena, given stage performances too. She has twenty years' experience in the field of journalism. She is a published author, and passionate environmentalist, social activist, she is helping women by providing them legal aid. She is serving society with her NGO Sarthak Disha which is working in the field of reproductive health of woman. Had been conducting workshops and distributing menstruation cups among underprivileged women. Working for empowerment and education of woman. For her efforts she has given several awards including prestigious Sarojini Naidu award.

CHAPTER 12

The Grace of
FORGIVENESS

Dr. Lorie A. L. Nicholas

I HATE YOU

The power behind three words can be filled with hurt and anger
and the impact of these emotions
messed with my head, and
weighed on my shoulders a ton

Although I never verbalised these words to you,
it was what I was feeling inside
I was a joke to you, someone you made fun of, but the hurt, the pain

I released as much as I could when I cried

I asked GOD how someone could who is also supposed to be a child of
GOD treat others in such an unscrupulous way?

Lying, Cheating, Stealing, being very critical and demeaning, acting like

I don't exist, but yet wanting me to stay?

No thank you, I have had enough,

I've got to preserve what is left of my heart, you see

I LOVE YOU

The power behind three simple words, that I now say to me.

Have you ever had your heart broken by someone whom you thought cared about   you? loved you? Or whom you thought was your good friend? It can be very hurtful when you realise that person never had your back.

Shaniya was a beautiful 28-year-old, African American sister. She had a head full of natural shoulder length hair that she sometimes wore professionally braided. Her eyes, mesmerising black and beautiful that held a shimmer of glimmer. Although Shaniya had a sexy curvaceous body, she often kept it covered up due to feeling self-conscious about her shape which often drew stares from both men and women, when not covered in oversized clothing. To her friends, they would always joke how Shaniya could get any man she wanted. But yet while a majority of Shaniya's friends were dating or married, Shaniya had spent the last 6 years working on her Bachelors and Masters Degree in Social Work which left very little time to date. Now that she was done with school, and had a great six figure job, Shaniya was open to dating. It did not take long before Darrell entered into her life. A handsome, African-American 32 year old male, with an Athletic build 6 foot 2 body frame. Darrell worked at a Car Dealership making $60,000 a year. After his basketball career did not evolve due to an injury, Darrell had visions of becoming a CEO of his own company. The relationship between Shaniya and Darrell seemed like a match made in Heaven for the first 12 months, Shaniya thought she had met the one, especially after Darrell started hinting at marriage. He did not seem to mind that she made more money than him. Shaniya covered 90 % of the bills after they moved in together 18 months into their relationship. She did not seem to mind covering a majority of the bills or fronting the money for Darrell's business startup funds. She believed in her man and felt that if she supported him now, he would be able to provide for them in the future.

One day, not long into the New Year's a lady Shaniya did not know approached her and slipped her a note and quickly walked away before Shaniya had even realised what had just happened. As Shaniya sat in her car, she slowly opened the note, palms beginning to sweat.

The first line of the note caught her attention "Your Man is My Sister's Man and they have three kids together and he has two kids with some other chick in another state, and heads up Sis, he's been dating someone you know, check out the photo enclosed.

So, if he's swooning you with that same old bull**** making you seem like you the best thing that ever happened to him, get ready to become a part of his already made family's."

Shaniya's head began to spin, she did not want to believe what she was reading and was scared to look at the photo. This has got to be a joke, a prank… any minute someone is going to jump out and say SURPRISE, a belayed April Fool's joke or something, some Reality TV show…but as Shaniya looked around there appeared to be no hidden TV cameras or people waiting to jump out and surprise her. She slowly pulled the picture out of the envelope, then gasped shouting "Janet ?" There in the picture was one of her close friend's exchanging a long passionate kiss with Darell, in a dress that she had borrowed from Shaniya.

Shaniya recalled that day Janet came overlooking in her closet for a sexy dress to wear for a romantic evening with a gentleman friend. Now it became clear why Janet never said his name and instead only referred to her gentleman friend as her "Secret Lover." Shaniya never imagined in a million years that the Secret Lover was actually her man Darrell. "That backstabber"- Shaniya screamed as people walked by her car shooting glances at her, alarmed by the screaming as Shaniya began talking loudly to herself. Janet was still up to her tricks of sleeping with other people's men, but she violated the Code of Honor, No Sleeping with Another friend's man. Shaniya 's heart sunk even deeper. Shaniya considered her close-knit circle of friends to be tight and to have each other's back. When she confronted Darrell about the note and the photo, he denied the information, he swore on his mother's grave, and as of the photo simply said "It wasn't me, but Wow I see how your head would be twisted. that guy sure does look like me."

Darrell disappeared out of Shaniya's life a week later. The information had turned out to be true. A few days later, Shaniya lost her six-figure job, due to assault charges that stemmed from an altercation between her and Janet about the relationship with Darrell. Now, Shaniya was left with No Man, No Job, and an outstanding debt that she would never be able to recoup, of $189,500.52. Money that had been used to help Darrell to build his dream business which ended up going nowhere. Shaniya found out that a significant amount of the money had been used to wine and dine his other women and buy them lavish gifts. In an instant, her life had been turned upside down.

Shaniya became angry, and bitter and was left asking "Why would he do this to me ?, How could he do this to us ?" Shaniya became deeply depressed. She neglected her hygiene and self-care, barely combing her once beautiful thick natural hair which had now become matted, falling out in clumps. She fed her pain through emotional eating.

Within a year Shaniya had packed on 100 pounds on her once curvaceous body. Her eyes no longer held a glimmer of light but were now dull and lifeless. She had utilised a significant portion of her savings toward the dream that Darrell never built. Afterall, at the time she was working and always thought that her six-figure income would supply for their needs. Without a job, and barely any income to cover 6 months' rent, Shaniya moved in with family. Through the constant attention and support from her family, Shaniya agreed to counselling and in time, learned to love herself again.

-Do you know a Shaniya in your life ?

-Perhaps you have had the unfortunate circumstance to have gone through some part of Shaniya's experience?

Either way, neither experience is fun.

The Wounds of Betrayal

When your heart is shattered by betrayal, deception and mistrust, this pain can cut deep, leaving scars that seem impossible to heal. One might experience sleepless nights, filled with replayed memories and unanswered questions. How could two people Shaniya loved so dearly betray her so profoundly? The bitterness that grew within her was like a poison, seeping into every aspect of her life. Shaniya learned that she had to find a way to forgive, not for the sake of the people who had betrayed her, but for her own peace of mind. Forgiveness, she realised, was not about condoning the acts but about liberating herself from the chains of bitterness and resentment.

The Journey to Forgiveness

Forgiveness is an eleven-letter word that carries an immense amount of emotional weight. To forgive means to cease feeling anger or resentment toward someone. However, forgiveness is not often easy to do. Forgiveness is a journey, often beginning with the acknowledgment of pain. It is essential to recognise and validate the hurt before one can move toward healing. For Shaniya, this meant allowing herself to fully feel the anger, sadness, and betrayal. She needed to confront these emotions, not suppress them or act out on them in an inappropriate manner through self-harm or displaced anger.

Shaniya decided to seek counselling. She began therapy and was guided on how to address her emotions. Shaniya was also introduced to journaling and was encouraged to write letters to her ex-boyfriend and former friend, letters she would never send. In these letters, Shaniya poured out her heart, expressing her pain, anger, bitterness, and the love that once existed between them. Writing became a cathartic release, helping her to process her emotions and gain clarity.

Shaniya's journey is not unique. Unfortunately, there are countless individuals both men and women who have faced the challenge of forgiveness after a very painful and emotionally charged relationship. Their stories, like Shaniya's serve as hope and wisdom, illuminating the path for others to be able to forgive and heal.

Remember, forgiveness is not about the other person; it is about freeing yourself from the burden of anger and bitterness. It is about reclaiming your power and choosing to live with an open heart.

The Role of Empathy

Empathy plays a crucial role in the process of forgiveness. It allows us to see beyond our pain and attempt to understand the humanity in those who have wronged us. Empathy does not excuse the behaviour but offers a perspective that can help us to open the door to forgiveness. For instance, we might find that this person struggles with a number of insecurities and a severe lack of confidence yet portraying that they have it all together. They find comfort in being demeaning and critical to others, giving a false belief that they are better or deserving of hurting someone else make themselves feel better.

Empathy also extends to oneself. Forgiving yourself for past mistakes is often one of the hardest things to do. The guilt and regret of feeling that the person made you look like a fool and enjoyed taking advantage of your time, your money, and your kindness. Learning to forgive yourself takes time. You feel unsure of yourself due to having trusted too easily and for not seeing the red flags warning of danger. Self-forgiveness is a very critical step in the healing journey, allowing yourself to release the self-blame that often weighs us down.

The Healing Power of Letting Go

The next phase of Forgiveness is Letting Go. It requires a conscious decision to release the hold that past hurts have on our lives. Letting Go is not about forgetting but about choosing peace over pain and not replaying these movies in our mind.

It is important to realise that holding onto anger only hurts you, and often prevents you from fully enjoying life and moving forward. Similar to the symbolic act previously discussed of writing letters to those who have hurt you, ad never mailing them, an additional step can be after reading them out loud, ripping them up, or burning the letters, watching as the flames consume the words, transforming them into ash. As the papers burn, take a deep breathe to feel a sense of release, a weightlifting off your shoulders, and state a positive affirmation affirming a new beginning.

Although this act will not erase the past, it can mark a new beginning, a fresh start, getting you prepared to move on, to embrace life with an open heart and to welcome new experiences and relationships without the shadow or baggage of past hurts.

Moving Forward

As you begin to take these healing steps toward forgiveness, the storm will clear, and the first rays of sunlight will break through the clouds. You will begin to feel a sense of inner peace that you might not have felt in a long time.

It is important to understand that the journey of forgiveness is an ongoing process' It is also important to give yourself credit that you have taken the most important steps of this journey – acknowledging the pain, seeking support, practicing empathy, engaging in healing, embracing self-forgiveness and learning to move forward.

As you move forward, let your pain turn into strength. Understand that the power to heal and move forward lies within you and that by choosing forgiveness, you are choosing to live a life filled with peace, love, and joy. As you read these words, may you find the courage to embark on your own journey of forgiveness, to heal the wounds of your past, and to embrace the beauty and love and the power of strength that lies inside of you, opening your heart to a wonderful future that lays ahead of you.

Handling Money Betrayals and Financial Loss

Financial betrayals and losses can be just as devastating. These situations often leave individuals feeling angry, and betrayed, as a result of the loss of the financial stability and security they once had. In Shaniya's story she was severely impacted. Therefore, along with having to recover from the pain of a relationship, she must also resolve to deal with how to handle money betrayals and financial loss, and be able to pursue forgiveness in this area as well,

What follows are some tips to receive guidance and forgiveness in terms of addressing money betrayals.

Understanding the Impact of Financial Betrayal

Money betrayals include the reality of financial loss; along with the impact of the loss of trust when it comes to money and personal relationships. The emotional toll can include feelings of anger, betrayal, shame, and anxiety about the immediate future. It is crucial to acknowledge these emotions as a legitimate response to one's current situation. Ignoring or suppressing them can prolong the healing process and delay the ability to get back on track financially.

Five Steps to Handle Financial Betrayal

1.   Acknowledge Your Emotions:

The first step in handling financial betrayal is to acknowledge the emotions it brings. It's natural to feel hurt, angry, and very disappointed. Allow yourself to experience these emotions without judgment. Writing in a journal or talking to a trusted friend or therapist can help process these feelings.

2.   Assess the Financial Damage:

Take a clear, objective look at the financial impact of the betrayal. Assessing the damage involves understanding exactly what has been lost and what the implications are for your financial situation. This step is essential for creating a plan to move forward.

3.   Seek Legal and Financial Advice:

Depending on the nature of the betrayal, seeking legal or financial advice may be an option. Consulting with a lawyer can help determine if there are any legal actions you can take to recover some of the losses. A financial advisor can assist in restructuring your finances and creating a plan to regain stability.

1.   Develop a Recovery Plan:

Create a practical and achievable plan to recover from the financial loss. This might include finding new sources of income, budgeting or re-evaluating financial goals. Having a clear plan can provide a sense of control and direction in the midst of an emotional financial recovery.

2.   Communicate Boundaries and Expectations:

If the person who betrayed you is still part of your life, it's crucial to establish clear boundaries and communicate your expectations moving forward. This step is vital for protecting yourself from future betrayals and rebuilding trust, if possible, and continue to proceed with caution. Seek help if you begin to have concerns regarding financial abuse.

Handling financial betrayal and loss is a deeply personal journey that requires patience, resilience, and a commitment to healing. By acknowledging your emotions, seeking professional guidance, developing empathy, and engaging in healing rituals, you can navigate the path to forgiveness. Self-forgiveness and setting clear boundaries are essential steps in moving forward and healing from money wounds left from an emotionally toxic relationship of betrayal.

So as we get ready to review the 7 Phases of Forgiveness, be sure to incorporate the five steps in the forgiveness of money betrayals if this section also applies to your situation.

Seven Phase Action Tips For Healing Through Forgiveness

The following is a recap of the visual representation of the Phases of Forgiveness, depicting the stages one might go through in their journey towards healing and moving forward. Also included is an affirmation, to help support you through your journey of Forgiveness, however, feel free to get creative and develop your own.

The 7 Phase Cycle of Forgiveness

1. Acknowledgment of Pain

2. Seeking Support

3. Empathy Development

4. Healing Rituals

5. Self-Forgiveness

6. Letting Go

7. Moving Forward

Each phase is interconnected, reflecting the continuous and ongoing nature of forgiveness. Feel free to utilise this abbreviated guide to navigate your own path to forgiveness.

1.　Acknowledgment of Pain

Affirmation: "I honour my feelings and give myself permission to feel the pain.

My emotions are valid, and I acknowledge them with compassion."

The first step in healing through forgiveness is to acknowledge the pain and accept that it is a valid response to being hurt. Recognise and validate the pain and hurt experienced. This initial step involves allowing yourself to fully feel and understand the emotions associated with the betrayal or harm done. Allow yourself to feel the full range of emotions without judgment.

2.　Seek Support and Guidance

Affirmation: "I am worthy of support and understanding. I seek and accept the guidance I need to heal and grow."

Forgiveness is a challenging journey, and seeking support from a therapist, counsellor, or trusted family member or friend can provide the guidance and encouragement needed to navigate this path. Having someone to talk to can provide new perspectives and emotional support, helping you navigate through your feelings and experiences.

3.　Practice Empathy

Affirmation: "I open my heart to understanding and empathy. I choose to see the humanity in others, even when they have hurt me."

The Book On Forgiveness

Try to understand the perspective and humanity of the person who hurt you. This does not excuse their actions but recognising that everyone has flaws and is capable of making mistakes might help you to view them differently.

4.   Engage in Healing Rituals

Affirmation: "I engage in healing rituals that help me release the past. Each act of letting go brings me closer to inner peace."

Create rituals that symbolise letting go of the past. This could be writing letters you never send, performing a symbolic act like burning the letters, or creating other activities that helps you to process and release these negative and painful emotions.

5.   Embrace Self-Forgiveness

Affirmation: "I forgive myself for any role I may have played. I release self-blame and embrace self-compassion and growth."

Forgive yourself for any role you may have played in the situation, whether it was trusting too easily, not seeing the red flags or ignoring the warning signs. Self-forgiveness is crucial in that it allows you to release self-blame and guilt, which are often significant barriers to moving forward.

6.   Letting Go

Affirmation: "I consciously choose to let go of past hurts. I free myself from the burden of pain and open my heart to new possibilities."

Make a conscious decision to release the hold that past hurts have on your life. This step involves accepting that what happened cannot be changed and choosing to focus on your present and future.

7.   Moving Forward

Affirmation: "I embrace my future with an open heart and mind. I am resilient, and I move forward with hope, strength, and joy."

Embrace the future with an open heart, free from the burden of past pain. This final stage is about integrating the lessons learned from the experience and using them to build a healthier, more positive outlook on life.

Each of these 7 Phases in this cycle is crucial for the process of forgiveness and healing. They are interconnected, meaning that progress in one area can facilitate growth in another. By understanding and working through each of these stages, individuals can find a path to inner peace and emotional freedom. The affirmations that are included are designed to support you through each phase of the forgiveness process, providing encouragement and a positive mindset as you heal and grow. Remember, forgiveness is not about condoning the betrayal but about freeing yourself from the burden of resentment and reclaiming your peace and well-being.

Closing: A Poem of Forgiveness

You hurt me deep, I felt the sting,
A broken trust, a painful thing.

But now I see, to heal my heart,
I must forgive, to make a start.

I cried, I raged, I lost my way,
Yet here I am, with more to say.

I choose to let the anger go,
And find the peace I used to know.

I understand, we're flawed and real,
In empathy, my wounds can heal.

Forgiving you, I free my soul,
In letting go, I become whole.

I forgive myself for all the pain,
For trusting deep, for hopes in vain.

Now moving on, my heart is clear,
With strength and love, I persevere.

7 PHASES OF FORGIVENES

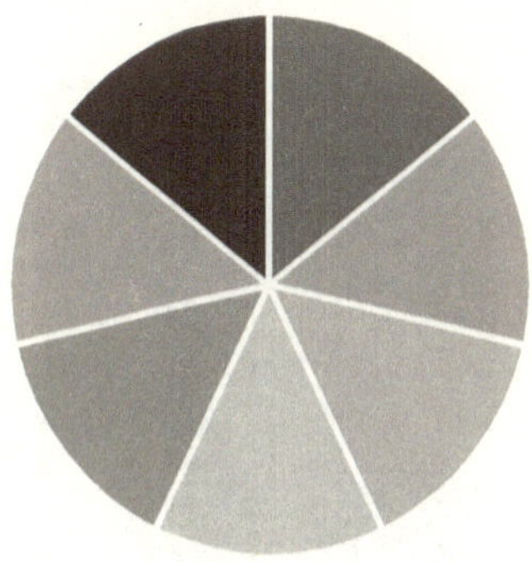

- Pain
- Guidance
- Empathy
- Healing
- Self-Forgiveness
- Letting Go
- Moving Forward

The Book On Forgiveness

About the Author:

Lorie A. L. Nicholas, Ph.D, CFEI, AFC has an extensive background in counselling, teaching, and research. She has presented at many conferences and has conducted a variety of workshops and trainings. Dr. Nicholas holds a doctorate in Clinical Psychology, is a Certified Financial Education Instructor and an Accredited Financial Counselor.

CHAPTER 13

A Sister's Journey From
ACCEPTANCE to REDEMPTION

Phyllis A Nunn

Forgiveness

The most critical component of self-love and sustainable strength everyone needs to master their life's journey. It is the key to freedom and enduring peace that will ultimately set you free.

Forgiveness is the fortifying foundation of personal growth that leads to understanding and relationship reconciliation when tangible solutions are not enough to settle supposed irreconcilable differences.

When individuals open their hearts to forgiveness, it opens their minds to self-love. It's a beautiful process when you can cultivate and infuse positivity with healthy relationships once thought unsalvageable. Forgiveness can also help foster a sense of worthiness and acceptance when your inner beliefs align with your thoughts that translate into action.

The act of forgiveness and self-compassion also plays a vital role in building resiliency, enabling individuals to navigate and overcome challenges with greater ease.

Equally important is self-forgiveness. By letting go of past grievances, you'll release yourself from harboured resentments that led to unfulfilled dreams. Give yourself time and space to unlock mental and emotional barriers inhibiting you from achieving your goals and aspirations.

Incorporating forgiveness strategies into your daily routine can promote inner peace, reduce stress, and pave the way for personal transformation. Forgiveness empowers individuals to transform limiting beliefs into stepping stones for continuous improvement in their newly designed reality. When you take time to forgive and reason with others from a position of love, you'll find your thoughts and your mind aligned in harmonious peace. Once you begin taking charge of your thoughts and your actions with an open heart, willing to forgive not only out of necessity but out of enduring love you'll see profound changes in your life.

The Book On Forgiveness

My greatest test of forgiveness occurred a few weeks ago after the death of my closest sister Karen. It was then I discovered I wasn't as powerless as she'd led me to believe. We nurtured each other's goals and dreams over the years, but our relationship became strained and contentious during the last three years of her life.

Phyllis Nunn and Karen Nunn Luney, 2022

Karen died June 7, 2024. Our relationship had become one of contentious disharmony wrought with misunderstandings and pain. Cancer is not an easy venture knowing it will eventually be the cause of your demise. All my siblings knew the pathology of her disease, but I believe that she hid the severity of her condition until she could no longer.

I've tried to understand her pain, her desires through the years, but as her health declined, so did aspects of our relationship. As I was pursuing holistic health studies, she was beginning to lose her ability to write with the most beautiful penmanship imaginable. The strained chasm of separation broadened as our meetings became shorter and wrought with challenging questions laced with truth and angst. In her presence, I often wondered, 'Why do I even try?' but I continued to help her despite her rather harsh treatment. I'm still trying to figure it out, but I guess it all boiled down to one single word... love. Though riddled with pity and unshakeable sorrow neither could escape, my actions and care were given out of love.

Forgiveness was difficult to embrace. We spoke of her condition lightly, but we tried to communicate as normal as possible until the end.

I think we tend to mask true emotions when we allow relationship roles to mature out of familial connection or need. Not to say that's the best solution, but it is what it is.

After years of well-defined roles—she the all-knowing big sister social worker and I the younger former actor who couldn't possibly be mature enough to coach and heal without her blessing—we drifted into different behaviours, and we often used aggression to relate to each other. We both had changed. The dynamics of the relationship had changed and there was no going back.

She challenged me at every encounter making it hard to forgive her, but I always did. I never understood how she gave so much love to the students she helped throughout the years at a Jefferson County Public School but reserved little compassion for me. Karen worked full-time three months before she passed. Seeing her struggle to live made me forgive her even more despite the harsh words she would reserve for me. I let her believe she was the victor of every disagreement knowing it would give her

Phyllis at the office

control of something. She was the ultimate puppet master and I the puppet, or was I? In the end, she finally gave me countless memories to cherish during the last few hours of her life. She loved me. That's all that matters now. She let me go, even when I didn't know she was gone. Thank you, Karen, for the good days and the bad. Thank you for teaching me how to think and to see life through your eyes. You're free now. No more pain. I forgive you. Thank you for forgiving me. I understand why.

Was the relationship challenging? Unequivocally yes. Would I have wanted our last days together less trying? One will never know.

My life with Karen will always be an exercise in forgiveness and futility, but one that gifted me with renewable hope and gratification for my life to come.

Today, I'm living life on my terms with God driving my choices. Truthfully, I didn't always consult God before making a life-altering decision. Karen's cancer-ridden logic was clouding my judgment. Good and bad. I relinquished my power to Karen, but I'm no longer shackled by her insecurities and fears that crippled my growth. My mind feels free and clear to navigate the rest of my life on my own terms. I had to forgive myself because the God I serve can restore health and longevity when you believe and commit to a servant mindset for others.

Over these past few weeks, I have begun taking more chances and have stopped giving my time to those who do not share my zeal for life. I always knew I held the keys to the many gifts God has bestowed upon me, but I'm doing my utmost to use these gifts and not put them aside as I have done for so long.

If you remember nothing from my story, please try to spend time with loved ones without judgment or waste time trying to convince others of your worthiness. All you need is God's grace to lead your thoughts, words, and deeds. God wants us to forgive each other and temper our words. Endless possibilities await you when you set your sites on impacting the world and not inflicting pain on the helpless.

Luke 9 speaks of "Dying to self..."

The purpose of sharing my story and my sanity, is to help you learn from my mistakes and to let go of petty arguments that are fleeting and less mendable with time. It means letting go of the old self, not winning every argument, and valuing the time you have left with another.

As I put on my new suit of self-reliance and self-forgiveness, I feel free to move forward with confidence and mindfulness to achieve greater heights in personal growth and development. My old self, the one who listened to my sister's advice and misdirection that was not in accordance with God's will for my life, has been traded in for one with hope for tomorrow that anything is possible when consulting God first and following his guidance.

Even though we spoke of God's divine intervention and direction for our lives, there was always something holding us back from moving into the positive realm of forgiveness and acceptance of each other's individuality.

I'm still working on why that aspect of the relationship was hard to remedy. I'm sure I'll figure it out one day.

Now, let's dive into the actionable steps I took toward establishing a mutually sustainable relationship filled with forgiveness. There are five promising steps that lead to forgiveness that are applicable in most personal and professional relationships. These steps require continuous improvement and accountability to yield the best results.

Key 1: Clarity of Purpose

Scripture Basis: Ephesians 4:32 (NIV) - "Be kind and compassionate to one another, forgiving each other, just as in Christ God forgave you."

Actionable Steps:

1. ***Understand the Purpose:*** Reflect on the purpose of forgiveness—to restore peace and relationships, and to emulate Christ's forgiveness. I needed the right mindset before beginning conversations with my sister which was often overlooked. The relationship was often contentious when I walked into the room because we never re-established clear boundaries. I was always the little sister and she the older, more self-righteous, and knowledgeable one who found it difficult to relinquish

birth right status.

2. ***Pray for Guidance:*** Seek God's help FIRST to gain clarity on the need for and importance of forgiveness in your life and of others. After settling yourself, forgive your presumed nemesis.

3. ***Identify the Hurt:*** Write down the specific grievances and hurts

that need forgiveness. You may find blame has your name attached.

4. ***Set Intentions:*** Clearly state your intention to forgive, both to yourself and in your prayers. Be sincere. God knows your heart and your level of commitment to remedy the relationship.

5. ***Practice listening:*** "Listen with the intent to understand." Steven Covey. "Think. Breathe. Listen before responding." Phyllis Nunn

Key 2: Focus on Healing

Scripture Basis: Colossians 3:13 (NIV) - "Bear with each other and forgive one another if any of you has a grievance against someone. Forgive as the Lord forgave you."

Actionable Steps:

1.   **Shift Your Focus:** Instead of focusing on the pain, focus on healing and moving forward. This one takes courage and maturity, especially in fatal situations. Timely patience is the author of transformative recovery.

2.   **Meditate on Scripture:** Regularly read and meditate on scriptures about forgiveness and healing. Your spiritual health deserves peaceful resolve.

3.   **Positive Affirmations:** Use to reinforce your decision to forgive and heal. Practice daily. I use an action faith board with scriptures linked to my actionable steps. I don't use vision boards because a vision without action is dead.

4.   **Seek Support:** Join a support group, talk to a spiritual mentor, or secure an accountability partner to help keep your focus on healing.

Key 3: Observation - What to Look For

Scripture Basis: Matthew 5:23-24 (NIV) - "Therefore, if you are offering your gift at the altar and there remember that your brother or sister has something against you, leave your gift there in front of the altar. First go and be reconciled to them; then come and offer your gift."

Actionable Steps:

1.   **Observe Your Emotions:** Notice your emotional reactions when you think about the person or situation.

2.   **Identify Triggers:** Recognise what triggers negative feelings and make note of the emotions it caused.

3.   **Practice Empathy:** Try to see the situation from the other person's perspective.

4.   **Look for Change:** Observe any changes in your feelings towards the person or situation over time.

Key 4: Resolving Differences

Scripture Basis: Matthew 18:15 (NIV) - "If your brother or sister sins, go and point out their fault, just between the two of you. If they listen to you, you have won them over."

Actionable Steps:

1.   **Communicate Openly:** Have an honest conversation with the person you need to forgive, if possible.

2.   **Express Your Feelings:** Clearly express how their actions affected you.

3.   **Listen Actively:** Listen to their side of the story without interrupting or judging.

4.   **Seek Reconciliation:** Work together to find a resolution that acknowledges and addresses the hurt.

The Book On Forgiveness

Key 5: Validation and Revalidation of Forgiveness

Scripture Basis: Luke 6:37 (NIV) - "Do not judge, and you will not be judged. Do not condemn, and you will not be condemned. Forgive, and you will be forgiven."

Actionable Steps:

1.   Self-Reflection: Regularly reflect on your feelings to ensure you have genuinely forgiven.

2.   Check for Resentment: Notice if feelings of resentment or bitterness resurface and address them immediately.

3.   Reaffirm Your Forgiveness: Periodically reaffirm your decision to forgive through prayer and meditation.

4.   Apply Forgiveness Daily: Make forgiveness a daily practice, extending grace to yourself and others.

Applying Forgiveness Strategies to Remain in a State of Forgiveness

The Book On Forgiveness

Scripture Basis: Philippians 3:13-14 (NIV) - "Brothers and sisters, I do not consider myself yet to have taken hold of it. But one thing I do: Forgetting what is behind and straining toward what is ahead, I press on toward the goal to win the prize for which God has called me heavenward in Christ Jesus."

Actionable Steps:

1. Daily Prayer: Start each day with a prayer asking for the strength to forgive and let go of past hurts.

2.   Scripture Reading: Integrate daily reading of forgiveness scriptures into your routine.

3.   Journaling: Keep a forgiveness journal where you write down your journey, progress, and prayers.

4.   Mindfulness: Practice mindfulness and meditation to stay present and avoid dwelling on past grievances.

5.   Acts of Kindness: Perform acts of kindness towards those you have forgiven to reinforce your decision.

By incorporating these steps and grounding them in scripture, you can embark on a transformative journey toward forgiveness, healing, and peace.

Why did I feel so compelled to forgive so easily, and yet feel so badly about myself?

I had allowed myself to die to self when I tossed my emotions aside, leaving the door open to forgive or walk away. I chose to stay and not walk away when she needed me most. Remember, no one can make you feel negatively about yourself without your permission. It was then I began to heal.

This exploration of forgiveness is allowing me to move forward with less fear and more determination to make wiser decisions based on my spiritual input rather than relying on advice from those who haven't walked my journey. It's actually rather freeing to know I'm standing in my truest definition of independence with no one's validation except my own. I pray you reach that level of self-acceptance to reach greater heights in your personal and professional careers.

Life is a journey. Not a destination. Trust your gut. You are more courageous than you know.

About the Author:

Phyllis A Nunn is a well-respected author, speaker, and Certified Trauma-Informed Trainer for the Kentucky Cabinet for Child and Family Services. She is also a highly sought-after Neuromuscular Massage Practitioner for the Veterans Administration Community Care Network and Department of Labor Workers Compensation Program. Phyllis specialises in delivering behavioural and physical rehabilitation therapies that calm the central nervous system, boost circulation, and reduce inflammation. She is the proud mother of one son, Joshua Marvin, currently pursuing his doctoral degree in Biology from Rensselaer Polytechnic Institute in Troy, New York. Her favourite scripture: Ecclesiastes 9:10 "Whatever your hand finds to do, do it with all your might, for in the grave, where you are going, there is neither working, nor planning, nor knowledge, nor wisdom."

CHAPTER 14

The power to
FORGIVE through FAITH

Alicia J. Alexander, Msl

2 Corinthians 10:3-5, New King James Version

[3] For though we walk in the flesh, we do not war according to the flesh. 4 For the weapons of our warfare are not carnal but mighty in God for pulling down strongholds, 5 casting down arguments and every high thing that exalts itself against the knowledge of God, bringing every thought into captivity to the obedience of Christ.

Youth is the age when regard for persons of authority develops. Youths learn how to respect authority appropriately. What happens when an adult authority figure violates a young person's ability to respect through improper behaviour? This is my story of how I learned to forgive an adult authority figure who molested me. I will reveal how I acquired the power to forgive. The Power to Forgive is not only the title of this story but also it is the God-given weapon to irradicate hurt from within the soul. The soul of a human being is where the mind, will, and emotions are housed. In the soul, hurt can cause pain to the body, especially in the joints. The saving Grace is to feed your spirit life-giving, redeeming words that restore your soul as shown in Psalm 23:3.

It was a bright, sunny day, and my siblings and I were home alone. The doorbell rang and there stood a recognisable figure, a respectable, authority figure, close to my family. I opened the door. He stepped in and within minutes my life changed from happy and youthful to disturbed and wondering what I did wrong to deserve such evil to happen to me. I took a vow of silence since I had no one to talk to, I thought not even my Mum would believe me that this man came to her home to sexually violate her daughter. I promised myself and God that I would keep my mouth shut unless I discovered that he did the same thing to another person. You may ask, why in God's creation would I promise myself such a thing? Honestly, because I felt I had no one to talk to. You might say, what about your Dad? My Dad died when I was young, age 6 to be exact.

I believed there was not one person who would believe me over this authority figure. My life changed. The only solace I had was to read my Bible in my room alone.

The relationship that I had with my brother and sister changed. Because I was deeply injured by this man's actions toward me. I felt that I became the family's black sheep so that they could have special privileges especially, through this man's graces.

Reading the Bible became more than a religious expression, it became my lifeline. I found peace in its pages. I attended church with my family: my Mum and siblings. However, it was in the confines of my bedroom that I knew Jesus loved me and I was okay. Seven years later I discovered that this man violated a young lady that was my friend. By this time, I was no longer a youth. As an adult, I remembered my vow and I decided that I would speak up to my friend's defence. I may not have had someone to confide in when it happened to me but, I sure was not going to be silent and allow my friend to suffer the way I did seven years ago. Did I use the power to forgive? I did. Yet, I did not fully understand how to forgive the man who violated my innocent trust in authority figures. All I knew was that I had to clear my heart of the negativity and the yuck that I felt. I wielded my God-given weapon of forgiveness for the first time. The result of me helping my friend was clarity in my perception of people. I could tell you who was the evildoer and who was the righteous. Regardless of the career of the man who violated my friend and myself, he was a very twisted man who deserved to be dealt with to the fullest extent of the law. However, that man was not condemned. My friend and I realised that man, the authority figure, had God to deal with. Without the power to forgive, we would have missed out on so much life.

As the years went passed by, I grew stronger in my faith. I became more confident in God's love for me and those close to me. At the age of 25, I married. My husband and I moved to Manassas, VA. It was there that I encountered Living Faith Ministries International. The Pastors were so real and they taught the Bible with so much life.

I got free from everything that had hurt me in my past. It was here that I learned about Truth which made me free, as stated in John 8:32, NKJV.

John 8:32, New King James Version
32 And you shall know the truth, and the truth shall make you free.

Through the teaching of Living Faith Ministries International, I learned I was forgiven and loved by God: The Father, Jesus, the Son, and The Holy Spirit. Most importantly, it was not my fault what happened to me. It was that man's sin, not mine. Knowing this truth as an adult made me free enough to fully forgive him and let go of the evil feelings I had within me. I realise at this very moment that God loves me so much that he set me free by allowing me to move to Virginia, a Lovers' state, and encounter true godly love which made me free from every evil Satan intended me to experience through this man's violation.

Today, I can share this story without fear, and I am confident I am loved by God, who empowers me to love others as I am loved. The hurt is gone and now, I know what Truth is in my daily life. I have the confidence to know what it means truly to have the power to forgive. I know I have been given authority in the name of Jesus and that I have an eternal godly family, as stated in Luke 10:19, 20, NKJV.

Luke 10:19-20, New King James Version

19 Behold, I give you the authority to trample on serpents and scorpions, and over all the power of the enemy, and nothing shall by any means hurt you. 20 Nevertheless do not rejoice in this, that the spirits are subject to you, but rather rejoice because your names are written in heaven." Personally, I feel that understanding the Word of God, The Holy Bible, allows a person to be free of all of Satan's schemes and deceit. God is love. God wants his creation: male and female whole, free of anything that does come from love.

Hence, when the enemy of our souls concocts schemes to do us damage, such as molestation or any other hurt. God says this is my child, not only will I heal him or her but also, I will give them double for their trouble. I have given them my Word and I watch over my Word to perform it, as written in Jeremiah 1:12, NKJV.

Jeremiah 1:12, New King James Version

[12] Then the Lord said to me, "You have seen well, for I am ready to perform My word"

The power to forgive is a God-given weapon that wields a powerful blow to enemy-built strongholds. It is the strategy to heal a person from the deepest hurt and give them the freedom to live again. If you are reading this testimonial of how a youth can be healed of a sexual violation against their innocence, and you have experienced this same kind of hurt, I recommend praying to God and reading Psalm 23 or a passage of the Bible that the Holy Spirit leads you to read. Allow me to share that the restoration of your being is not always immediate, but the healing starts when a person decides to use the power to forgive to let go of the feelings of hurt and pain. God's love is the healing element. I admonish you to forgive and let it go. Healing and restoration are better than revenge. Trust me! Better yet, trust God.

God's Word, The Holy Bible is full of life-giving truth that when a person reads it, it delivers you from every spiritual attack against the human soul or body. Supplying the human spirit with Truth from God's Word, The Holy Bible, is the most freeing thing a person can do to heal their entire being. The power to forgive is real especially when you entrust the pain and hurt that you may experience to God. Remember, God did not design you to experience this hurt or pain. It was orchestrated by Satan. No, not the being in a red suit and carrying a pitchfork but a fallen archangel whose plan is to deceive as many people as possible and to take them to hell with him. This diabolical plot has been exposed by God's Truth.

As you read this story, if you wish to know who God is and you want to experience his love, then say this prayer or just talk to God about whatever you wish to say to him.

Talk to God as if he is in the same room at this moment with you because he is.

<u>A Prayer to Heal</u>

Heavenly Father, your Word says, "You love me."

At this moment, I choose to believe this truth.

I believe in my heart and I confess with my mouth,

I believe God you love me and you do not want me to hurt

anymore or experience pain any longer.

I hand you every pain and hurt, now.

Thank you that you heal me and remove everything that is not love far from me.

I renounce every evil thought or action I have allowed to consume me due to the pain and hurt.

I accept Your love and ask You to minister Truth to me now,

In the name of Jesus, Amen.

Now that you began the healing process through prayer, I ask you to accept Jesus as Savior and Lord by saying the following words...

Heavenly Father,

Your word is near us, in our mouths and our hearts—the word of faith which we decree and declare. Lord, we confess with our mouths that Jesus is Lord and believe in our hearts that You raised Him from the dead. We believe Your promise that by faith, we are saved.

Lord, it is with our hearts we believe unto righteousness, and with our mouths, we make confession unto salvation. Your Word assures us that whoever believes in You will not be put to shame.

We thank You, Father, that there is no distinction between humanity, for You are the same Lord over all, and are rich to all who call upon You. We hold onto the promise that whoever calls on the name of the Lord shall be saved. In Jesus' name, we pray, Amen.

Now, that you have prayed this prayer, "Welcome to God's family." You are a new person! There are a few things that I want you to do to enforce your new life and to grow in your new forgiveness life. I confirm that if you intentionally do the following, you will live life to the fullest.

1.   Spend time with God by reading your Bible.

       a.   In spending time with God and His Word, you will receive love and learn what Truth and true love is.

       b.   The benefit of reading the Bible is to know you have a Heavenly Father who is for you and wants to lavish on you His goodness.

2.   Find a church or community centre that teaches The Bible or faith and is Holy Spirit-filled. You might be wondering, how will I know if this is the right place? The church leaders will be full of life and read God's Word. They will encourage you to bring your Bible and read it along with them, most importantly, the people will worship God with enthusiasm, joyfully and the church will be full of godly life.

3.   Attend this prayer house or community centre faithfully, for at least 50 weeks of the year. Faithful attendance of a Holy Spirit-filled church does something to the entire being. It makes you free in your Spirit, revives your soul, and keeps your body strong.

4.   Make friends with people who genuinely love God. These friends will be encouragers and faithful to God. They will encourage you to love God and to be faithful to God's calling on your life.

5.   Finally, enjoy your new life with God. You have a new life, now. All of the past is gone. Now, trust God with your entire being and listen to His Spirit in you to enjoy what He has given you... a new beginning through the power to forgive.

About the Author:

Alicia J. Alexander, MSL, is the Founder of Make A Difference Consulting in Pawtucket, RI. As an Appreciation Expert and a Certified Facilitator of The 5 Languages of Appreciation In The Workplace, she specialises in fostering authentic appreciation and harmonious work cultures. Ms. Alexander is a published author on the topic of Organisational Development and Change. She holds a Master of Science in Leadership from Grand Canyon University, and she is pursuing a Doctor of Education degree in Organisational Leadership with an emphasis on Organisational Development (qualitative research).

CHAPTER 15

CHAPTER 15

The intensity of
FORGIVENESS and TRANSFORMATION

Anju Sharma

When I think of the power of forgiveness and how it can transform individuals, the first story that I think of is a recollection by James Autry, from his childhood, of an event when his father demonstrated the power of transforming rage to compassion. The second is a more contemporary example of a former political prisoner, Venerable Sangharakshita, and comes from the ravages of the present day which we often see on our television screens. The third is an incredible, heartrending and transforming tale of Pumla Gobodo-Madikizela who listened to the confessions of a black South African, a former policeman to apartheid, who had committed unspeakable atrocities on the family of her friend and comrade, thus nurturing a remarkable restorative justice.

The very fact that political prisoners, such as Nelson Mandela of South Africa, in their difficult circumstances, were able to forgive and work with the very forces who had incarcerated them, is indeed admirable. Societies, such as the South African, the Rwandan and the Palestinian, have, through their times, used other expressive ways to express forgiveness and that acts to renew their humanity within. It is common to hear stories of forgiveness from such places. The good news is that we do not have to experience such extremes to make use of what we can learn from the experiences of those who emerged from their suffering, whole, healed and transformed. All of us have people and situations in our lives at many layers of significance that have called for deep forgiveness. These lessons enhance our understanding, skill and courage by providing guidelines, suggestions, practical methods of exercising forgiving - instead of the habit of choosing revenge or retribution.

Significance of Forgiveness

The act of forgiveness to me, is perhaps the most spiritual and divine quality that humans can express. It is an act of compassion and trust in oneself, freeing the individual and allowing a sense of inner healing. By experiencing forgiveness, individuals release their own spirit from the bindings and emotions that stand in the way of the ability to live a free, mature, and growth-oriented life. "Forgiveness is an inner act of compassion which cannot be forced," unknown. The significance of genuine forgiveness is not necessarily in the act itself, even though this act alone can result in physical and physiological healing. But the true significance is the altered state of being and new consciousness that individuals receive by offering and accepting forgiveness in their lives. For some, forgiveness is a way of acting, often a way of proving moral superiority to others. But there is a great deal of difference between this kind of forgiveness and the kind of forgiving that enhances relationships and moves individuals to a new level of consciousness.

When forgiveness is practiced genuinely, people have the ability to display a kind of grace, free of judgment, and reflect an unconditional spiritual flow. This process enables individuals to have a certain level of freedom and acceptance. However, true forgiveness takes time, a deep emotional process that can be met through stages of anger, loneliness, and grieving before reaching the final stage of letting go.

The Book On Forgiveness

In Buddhist centres and monasteries, the silence is held with strict discipline. Most communication is held anew every day with a series of hand motions. But in silence, my left ear picked up a very quiet, but distinct, rattling sound. Rhythmic, relentless, unwavering. My mind began to race around, trying to match this noise with something it had to be. "Surely, with millions of different pieces of life forms out there to create sound, surely a human wasn't persistent enough to actually follow me down to this room and, during the silence, shake a matchbox nonstop for over an hour. That would make no sense." "Maybe it's my own body - is my ear making my eardrum shake in a way that I can hear it?" I tilted my head, covered the ear, took a deep breath to un-pop my ears, but there it was, still rattling away. Then I had it. I had realised that what I was hearing was a snake.

The snake had found its way into my room and had coiled itself awake around the mosquito net I was renting. I was so far from my usual patterns back home that I had totally let down my guard with regard to this unaccustomed environmental danger. But my mind on a meditation retreat was like a ninja: it was ready for things other people would never suspect. Unreasonably calm, I decided to finish the rest of the meditation session before gently knocking my knees to signal that the teacher should come in to extract the unwanted guest. After all, if the snake had decided to come to a dharma talk, it deserved respect and my full attention. With the assistance of a broom, the snake was delicately swept out of the room, and I walked it out to the garden to begin its new life. That was the first time my forgiveness had been tested during that retreat.

Lessons Learned

What I've learned from my inner journey is that you have to be true to yourself and live by what you believe down in your deepest core. If you're trying to do what someone else dictates or thinks you should do, it just doesn't resonate with you, and you won't really believe in what you are doing or become a master at it. In fact, you'd find that you aren't happy doing it and get more and more upset or even physically ill. You must follow what your heart is guiding you to do. The first person we have to forgive is ourselves. I had to find a way to let go of what had happened to me and be at peace with it.

The Book On Forgiveness

I had to free myself from the emotional imprisonment I had locked myself in. The responsibility for this decision was left entirely in my own hands. There was no one who could force me to forgive, and there was certainly no one who could stop me from forgiving. That day when I first heard those words in my mind, I realised that I was the only one who could do anything about my predicament. I had choices to make, and they had to come from deep within me. At that moment, I gradually began to disentangle myself from the anger and hatred that had wrapped around my life. Only then was I able to start building something better for myself.

Reflecting on Insights

Immediately after this unprecedented experience, I pondered over what had just happened to me and tried to make sense of it. At that time, all that I could relate to, with all that I had read and understood about karma, was that forgiveness had just released a part of my negative karma. It was about how I had reacted to a similar situation that determined the result in any present moment sneak-attack at getting even. In sheer desperation of difficulty in confrontation with my consciousness, I had imploringly pleaded for help from any enlightened soul who was around, who was compassionate and understanding enough to calm me, to still the churning emotions in me. Shock and shame followed immediately, to be evaluated later continuously for learning that would fit in with the wisdom that could be sparkled out of the memory for all times.

Welcoming the opportunity to witness his sincerity in asking for forgiveness immediately heightened my compassion for him. Whether he was sincere or not was immaterial at that point. I felt delighted by the action, which I took as sincere.

Combining the feeling of delight and the feeling of heightened compassion, I found that my conscious mind that needed to think about the next steps or on what to say next was beginning to relent, dying a natural death. I became a total passive observer in this heated and confrontational challenge. My churning heart acquiesced with a pleasing finality the conflict was over. I was unassailably calm again and the initial periods of children rioting started to flow my being easing into acceptance on a higher and broader plane. The calm allowed new learning and realisations to temper out of the situation that was experience-created.

Inspiring Advice

I realised that the more positive and loving qualities that I have, the more positivity and love one could enjoy and experience. If you are facing a difficult situation, please hold on to your integrity and remain gentle.

Most importantly, be able to believe in the goodness of others; celebrate the good in others. If you are facing an unpleasant life experience, please remember, life is not about waiting for the storm to pass. It is about learning how to dance in the rain.

We create our own reality with what we persistently believe. Thus, never question the power of thought to get what one wants; don't forget to give and let others receive what they need. It is also a kind and gentle action to accept their gifts and help. This allows us to walk gently through our own lives, following our own path. It also heals, soothes, and brings comfort to our hurting world and people. The honesty, compassion, joy, and love that come to us also return to others as well. All in all, let's do good to feel great. I value my years of experience of changing classrooms, nurturing and influencing young people, especially teenagers. These lessons have shown me invaluable tools to cherish. These lessons are simple and powerful and are our foundation and strength in pursuing our dreams.

A Positive Message

The same as with the issue of humility, there are preconditions that being raised harmonising feelings and attitudes in a person. Fostering or trying to point out just kindness and honesty, to mention but two, implies removing such self-defensive aspects as ingratitude, hypocrisy, selfishness, or insensitivity, to mention just a few. A feedback mechanism makes functioning such values possible, which, in turn, generates a positive message the parents would like to leave in the world. Therefore, it works as a basic mechanism preventing gaps generally filled with hostile other mechanisms replacing positive values with negative ones. Such breeds revenge, against ingratitude, hypocrisy, selfishness, insensitivity, etc. A positive message would work here as a replacement or counter-weapon. Hence, a peace-promoting climate would help to make a more peaceful world, benefiting its every inhabitant. It all starts within the family.

Conclusion

In the final analysis, the more one moves toward forgiveness, the more one realises that the only journey to be made is the personal one. That is, forgiveness is somewhat of a lonely trek best made without feeling compelled by either internal or external strictures, or by contrary exhortations. It may be a long trek, especially for those who have been personally hurt by acquaintances, friends, or even strangers. The nature of the injury is ultimately less important than the choice one makes: a choice to forgive. And in choosing to forgive, there may be no more valuable journey than making a commitment to the self, a movement towards self-awareness that brings to light the sometimes-unfamiliar pathways of the human spirit.

Forgiveness would seem to be the renewed ability of an individual to act in a dignified, compassionate, and loving manner towards an individual who has behaved in an undignified, judgmental, and unloving fashion. Encounters with unbiased and unconditional kindness of the sort shown by Professor O'Driscoll are strongly supportive, but unfortunately rare. These positive and spontaneous instances of love remind victims of the transforming power they can bring to their pain.

The Book On Forgiveness

Yet the commitment to forgive is unarguably the most painful decision to make. The road not taken - not forgiving - is the road to prolonged suffering of the self. Each person's capricious journey towards forgiveness is as unpredictably unique as it is the purest of human experiences, conveying hope, courage, relief, and growth. Each encounter with genuine human warmth reaffirms our dubious certainties and uncertainties about our relationship to others.

About the Author:

Anju Sharma, a postgraduate from Delhi University, has dedicated over forty years to serving as a public intellectual and community leader. As Chairperson of the Pandit Tilak Raj Sharma Memorial Trust USA, she has tirelessly promoted the Hindi language and Indian culture in the USA. Her efforts have motivated and united the community, inspiring countless individuals and educating thousands. Anju Sharma's unwavering dedication has preserved ancient and specialized arts, ensuring they remain vibrant and accessible. Her impactful work continues to foster cultural appreciation and community cohesion, leaving a lasting legacy for future generations.

CHAPTER 16

SELF-FORGIVENESS
and the diverse paths of creating legacy
Aviella Aloha Gray

In the journey of self-forgiveness, we must confront the painful truth that our greatest act of survival often comes from the choices we regret the most. Dear younger me, I know you're grappling with the weight of expectations and the silent question of motherhood. Every choice that you have made up to this moment has protected you from many uncertainties with the potential to completely devastate the plans that you have made for your life. Having aged out of foster care, we struggle with trust due to past experiences. We don't feel confident in our ability to succeed in protecting ourselves, so how could we protect our children? We never have the necessary support or resources needed to fully accept or embrace the heroic role of a mom.

Our philosophy on motherhood is a reflection of our psychological development from our transition from girlhood to womanhood, growing up outside the safety of trusted people. A concept coined on a YouTube video sermon by Pastor Lachele Bryant of Inspired Life Ministries and our prayer partner in Christ. We cringe at the thought of what we would have to endure and resolve in a world where young ladies come into contact with more males than men. Our bodies have been violated and mistreated by family members, so called friends, individuals in authority and their gang members. We sometimes find it possible to forgive them but not ourselves. Because we know that we are the only common denominator in the sum total of our life experience, how can we not condemn ourselves in some way, on some level, in some circumstances for what we have or have not become. Right or wrong, crooked or straight. We are our own worst critic. But the bible says in Romans 8:1 "Therefore, there is no condemnation for those who are in Christ Jesus.

Let me first take you back down memory lane and then tell you about the journey ahead, the path you'll choose, and the peace you'll eventually find in your decision.

Let's begin with the moment when you came to know how your mother felt about her choice to marry your father and conceive you. You were around eight years old when she told you her truth. Having you, her child, was a mistake! She had her heart set on being a businesswoman and maybe transitioning into having her own business one day. She mentioned the name KAP&CO for the business. Each letter in the name represents the first name of our intermediate family, excluding both fathers with her initial position in last place before the "and company" description. I always wondered why she chose that position. She could have arranged it in a different order where she would be first and not the last. How peculiar! He was born first; we were born next and then the woman who sacrificed her all shows up behind us.

Our older brother was born eight years before our birth. His father was, shall I say, unkind to our mother and it left her scorned in many ways. We don't need to talk bad about another man's father here. The fact is, our brother grew up hating our mom, that is how he used to refer to her. He would say yo mama this, and yo mama that whenever he needed to reference her in conversation. He absolutely and completely held her responsible for his father's absence in the home. To him, she failed! My mother had no choice but to bear the brunt of her son's attitude about having minimal accessibility to his own father throughout most of his life growing up. Now we both know that we don't want to deal with that rubbish. Our parents split up causing us to be removed from the only house and home that we knew up until that point. We were considered a family of the middle class. Historically, being a middle-class family meant having financial stability, owning a home, affording higher education for children, and enjoying a comfortable standard of living.

It included steady employment, health insurance, retirement savings, and the ability to take vacations and participate in community activities.

Middle class families often experienced a sense of economic security and upward mobility, symbolising the American dream. That all came to an abrupt halt didn't it?

In a final desperate attempt to get us to stay in the home, our father will plead with us, and ask us not to go. However, our second-grade deductive reasoning ability will base the decision to leave a spacious three bedroom single family home with a driveway and garage, a full basement with a large front yard, fenced in backyard with a BBQ grill and a swing set with a slide on a simple needs assessment. Who feeds us, who talks to us and who hugs us the most? The answer to our question was then and still holds true to this day; our mother does. We answer our father by telling him we want to stay with our mother. In that moment we break his heart into puzzle pieces. I forgive you.

For him, it might feel like the ground that you stand on is being divided like the effects of a strong earthquake. It won't take much time before we begin to feel the wrath of father's anger. First he refused to pick up the phone when we called. Our letters are never acknowledged nor answered. He was intentionally ignoring us. Hatred stirs up conflict, but love covers over all wrongs. Proverbs 10:12

In about four years from the day we departed, from the inside of a juvenile detention centre, our father will receive a very important call from an assigned case worker. After the first ring, she will elect to place the call on speakerphone. And in this instance, he will answer the phone. But when he does, his response will change our understanding of what family really is. Specifically when asked to come to St. Louis, MO to pick us up after a reported sexual abuse and rumours of child neglect, the case worker will say to our father, "Mr. Moore, I have your daughter with me. She is about to go into the foster care system permanently if you don't come and get her.

A very awkward silence will persist for what seems like forever. And the first time we hear my father speak he will say, "I don't have a daughter"! Then he will promptly release the call on his end. And his decision will thrust us into the division of family services.

A circumstance that I can only explain to you as cruel and unusual punishment beloved. My well-being, our well-being meant absolutely nothing to him. The trajectory of our lives was in the power of his influence, and he straight up denied us. Instantly, we were placed in a jail cell until the social worker could find a bed for us. Hours went by. The bed was made of concrete.

It was freezing in the building and there was no blanket or pillow or anything to keep warm with.

Now, we have no choice but to grow up fast because our next stop will be emergency placement at a mental hospital where other kids our age are being treated with hard core pharmaceutical drugs. You will spend a good amount of time there over the course of 2 separate visits. They will eventually release you and place you with a foster family, and then transition you into a sequence of group homes that you will eventually age out of. You will have many nights to think about what you did when you denied your father his request. I forgive you. If you only knew that your decision to go with your mother would result in all that you would endure on your own, alone and in kiddie captivity, would you have made a different decision?

I know how hard it's been to forget about it and put the past behind us. But forgiveness is not about erasing our past, but about reclaiming our future with the boldness to accept our imperfections. In the cold dark of the night, you will sometimes wake up crying and calling out for a mom. You will question what it means to be a parent. What it means to be a mother. What it means to be loved. You will understand what it means to be abandoned. And you will wonder if you did something to break your parents up. If your birth was the mistake that changed your mother's life in a way that cost her everything, she ever wanted to achieve for herself. What if it cost her the sacrifice of her goals and dreams. You will recall our mother repeating the chant "do everything you want to do in life before you have children" over and over again. Because she had to work two jobs to put food in our mouths and clothes on our backs. She paid the mortgage to keep a roof over our head. And after working 16 hours in a day, she would have to come home and cook and clean." Do you think in her mind she was successful? Do you think that she was happy with her choice to be a mother?

Let's switch our focus to the journey ahead now. Fast forward to age 17. We decide that despite the odds we are going to be successful. Anything that looks like it will stand in the way of us achieving our goal will get side stepped with the quickness. First, we determine what success will look like for us. And for us, success was staying alive, staying out of jail, time management, having fun, travel and financial independence. We begin to take inventory of our actions. We intentionally put our minds on education and skills development for income generation and off of males that we affectionately refer to as two legged dogs. They notice our focus and try to distract us.

They approach us with ignorance and inquire about why we choose to be single.

Because we choose not to behave like several of the other girls that we used to call fast. Those girls were doing a lot of things that adults do, yet they were not adults. For example, they like drinking alcohol, having sex with multiple partners and only God knows what else. Males would make stupid remarks about us not having been pregnant yet saying things like, what's wrong with you? Or you must be crazy or gay! We do our best to pay them no mind but their words penetrate us from time to time. They are trying to steal our joy and disrupt our happiness. Placing value on things that don't actually have value in order to deter us from the things that do.

We are young but we are discerning. More and more students are popping up pregnant all around us. We can look around in different directions and observe the lives of the high school students who got pregnant at an early age. We can see that they don't appear to be happy. "Happiness is not something ready-made. It comes from your own actions." The Dalai Lama.

Our choices will protect us from unwanted outcomes. There is a thin line between success and failure. Success is not the key to happiness; Happiness is the key to success. If you love what you are doing, you will be successful." Albert Schweitzer So when you finally get out of the facilities version of foster care into a residential group home environment you will be different. Your speaking style will change, to reflect your new badass personality. We start to feel anxiety about making changes in our lives and the uncertainty that comes with it. We begin to feel isolated and lack motivation. Struggling with self-motivation and feeling disconnected

from supportive communities we realised that we, you and I Aviella, are all that we have. We go deep into thought about the whole situation as it slowly begins to overwhelm us.

Not every young lady or woman is born to this world to become a mother. Blessed are those who do, and blessed are those who choose not to.

We were born to produce wealth by becoming proficient in areas surrounding our spiritual gifts. We have several of them. One of which is the gift of giving. The gift of giving is the divine strength or ability to produce wealth and to give by tithes and offerings for the purpose of advancing the Kingdom of God on earth. But I know we have trust issues. We also have a fear of failure. And this fear of failure is preventing us from trying and conquering a lot of purpose-aligned obstacles and challenges that are designed to prepare us to walk in our purpose. You don't want to be a mother because you are worried about parenting challenges, proper housing in a safe environment and relationship instability. You know what it is for the people around you to give up on one another. You don't want to raise a child or children of your own in poverty with an absent father. You're not sure that you have the ability to do better than your own parents did with you because you think you don't have the resources available to be successful.

You haven't had much access to positive role models in this area so your psychology around this topic is completely understandable. I forgive you! Imagine a life where the act of forgiving oneself becomes the most radical and transformative step towards crafting a legacy. Your legacy can be built through the lives you touch, the dreams you inspire, and the positive change you foster, proving that there are many ways to make a lasting mark. Embracing the many avenues to legacy building allows you to understand that your influence and contributions hold the power to shape the future in profound ways.

The Purpose Driven Wealth Network is an entrepreneur membership organisation dedicated to inspiring and equipping individuals to achieve financial freedom and leave a meaningful legacy. For me this journey is deeply personal, as I channel my passion and energy into my businesses, treating them as my children. Through Urban-n-Island and my other ventures, I am crafting a legacy of empowerment, creativity and resilience. By guiding others on their path to wealth and purpose, I am not only building my own legacy but also planting the seeds of hope and transformation that will flourish for generations to come.

The road to self-forgiveness is paved with the unspoken struggles of those who think and choose to protect their future by sacrificing the dreams of their past. In the quiet moments of self-reflection, forgiveness emerges as the powerful force that reshapes our identity and fuels the creation of lasting legacy. You have to learn to select your thoughts the same way that you select your clothes everyday. This is a power you can cultivate. If you want to control things in your life so badly, work on the mind. That's the only thing you should be trying to control. A quote from the movie, Eat, Pray, Love

As I sit by the Ka'anapali ocean, the waves gently lapping at the shore, I find solace in the rhythm of the tides. Like the ocean my journey has been one of ebbs and flows, of choices made and forgiven. At this moment, I am at peace with the legacy I am still actively creating for us, knowing it is as vast and enduring as the sea itself.

In the end, I forgive myself for the paths not taken, and embrace the woman I have become. My legacy is a testament to the power of choice, the beauty of self-acceptance, and the strength found in forgiveness. To those reading my story, I invite you to reflect on your journeys. Embrace the choices that define you, forgive yourself for the paths not taken, and recognise the profound legacy you are creating with every act of love and kindness. May the Lord bless you and keep you and give you peace.

About the Author:

Aviella Aloha Gray is from Maui, she is a multi-talented entrepreneur, licensed insurance agent, and passionate financial educator. Founder of Urban-n-Island, she crafts luxurious island-inspired products and services. As a lead author in Gumbo for the Black Woman's Soul, Aviella shares her journey of resilience and creativity. With a background in Travel and Tourism Management, she excels in connecting people to culture and financial wellness. Aviella's signature clarity framework and energy aligned affirmations empower others to achieve sustainable wealth and legacy. She embodies love, purpose and visionary leadership in all her endeavours.

CHAPTER 17

PERSONAL insights
on FORGIVENESS

Dr. G.A. Asif Jamal

I have witnessed many sad and troubling stories and events that people have coped with innumerable permutations of agonising issues. These experiences have reshaped me intellectually, emotionally, spiritually, professionally, and in so many other ways. Strengthened by these experiences, I offer a way of wavering through aversive matter by looking into the multiple ways in which so many have overtaken the approach to confronting violation, injustice, hurt, and despair.

Not all encounters of hurt and injustice are similar, nor is my spirituality and forgiveness healing journey exactly the same as any other. Many aspects of my collaborative journey as a qualitative, narrative, holistic, and action-oriented researcher are included in and mostly underpin my understanding of being-in-the-world and my rich phenomenology of mind, spirituality, and forgiveness as experienced during my close. My journey tale starts where I have confronted some of the richest blessings from my mentors and mentors in my developmental-educational and training history. These blessings support my ongoing unfoldingness as I collaborate with so many others who teach me sub as I share, teach, and support them. Even the best of conceptual models and tools must be applied and discussed realistically, humanly, and rethought for the present moment-context inter-phenomena. Working closely with others has forced humility with whatever conclusions we draw, each time we draw them, and against any arrogance, rigidity, or dogma. This is an unfolding part of the story of developing and teaching justice and healing applications of spirituality and forgiveness processes. At no time can we ever have a final theory of mind, justice, forgiveness, or applied collaborative healing. We can only conceptualise and apply the best tools we have developed so far in our addressing each specific instance of each presentation, as guided by our totality of understandings.

Significance of Forgiveness in Personal Growth

If there is any emotion that is part of the life of every individual, it must be forgiveness. Man is a social being and he knows how to offend others and how to torment. By that, forgiveness becomes very important. To forgive is something that could not be easily explained. If one wants to know, consult those that are in conflict and have vulnerable feelings, and he or she might experience what the feeling of forgiveness is just like them. Highly educated professionals in domestic homes, schools, the greater number of religious institutions, and the society at large began only recently to show awareness in this area. But those who have forgiven have appeared throughout human history, often taking on the likeness of the statement of Lord Jesus himself.

No one that values his or her health will indulge in anger and bitterness because the individual is forgiven. Nursing such feelings in the heart can cause the body's hormones and the amount of adrenaline secreted to increase, the body can collapse much easier. Such an individual might never have a permanent smile. The individual must then forgive no matter the circumstances. Discrimination must not be allowed to blemish the eyes. The recent area of counselling psychology in mental health that gives a "nod of approval" is that of forgiveness. For that reason, institutions are providing more teaching, training, and practical experiences to make such firm as those of the Indian parents.

The Book On Forgiveness

Personal Experience

Forgiveness is at the heart of every healing journey, suiting our souls and spirits. Studies have confirmed the joy and peace that accompany it. However, giving up grudges does not come easily. Coming to terms with our suffering and being willing to lack all will to revenge put us in conflict with our own need for order, justice, and understanding. We resist extending ourselves to the wrongdoer and making use of this radical remedy for anger and hurt because of the pain involved in giving up our grievances and

resentments. Holding on to one's resentments seems right at the time, like the need to retaliate in road rage. We insist we are justified, but our righteous indignation and need for just deserts persist.

I find isolation and quarrelling bring out my worst. I become judgmental. My anger blinds me. When I stay in victim mode, my support group bears witness to my poor detached spirit as they strive to provide healing and understanding. Their intolerance of my smallness of spirit reminds me of what I know in my heart: at some point, I must confront my tormentors. Pretending it never happened is not an option. Morally, acknowledging them without a forgiveness ceremony does not make for a happy journey in this life. I am filled with disgust and self-loathing when I offend. I have learned the practice of forgiveness through my own anguish and from the example of prominent individuals who have managed to avoid the ultimate act of revenge in pursuit of a more enlightened path. Theirs are the guided journeys of which I want to be a part.

Forgiving a Childhood Friend

Although I recently defined forgiveness as a personal experience, focusing on one's own willingness to communicate through love, it is of interest to critically reflect on my previous definition with regards to a definition of forgiveness that pertains exclusively to a social matter. While exploring definitions of forgiveness, the aforementioned interchange with a friend came to mind. If forgiving a world full of wrongdoing is so difficult, how could a current friend pretend that "your tormentor" was no longer a human being to her friend and forgive if she didn't believe that part of herself had also shut off humanity?

Why did I struggle with the concept of forgiveness? Did I really want what I thought I wanted? After some personal exploration, I shared my concern with my friend.

Breast cancer took Charlotte's life. Often as fate would have it, events come full cycle and I must again consider how to transform a very personal journey into an academic commentary for those looking for forgiveness through understanding. During a recent academic debate, I mediated an argument between two academic scholars. The argument was about the definition of forgiveness. Their dispute was the impetus for my order of note cards. On the note cards, I am defining, of course, forgiveness. This task was not easily done. The assignment rekindles my personal discomfort with the idea of forgiveness. I remembered my initial hesitation. What was the personal quest on which I had certainly embarked when I initially decided to explore the concept of forgiveness? I decided that I wanted to learn more about forgiving and forgiveness. I learn best about things in which I have an interest or am concerned. Wow! Had I truly embarked on this journey?

Lessons Learned

Forgiveness is a process that is embedded in experiences where people change as a function of reconciling a transgression. In interpreting these lessons learned, we also address the issue of moral superiority that can accompany discussing forgiveness - an obvious potential consequence of people examining their own experiences of forgiving. It is both accurate and tempting to portray forgiveness as the victory of good over evil, yet in reality the experience of forgiving is more complicated than that. It is not always apparent right away that forgiving is what should or could be done. The journey to forgiveness is not easy, nor is it one that everyone is prepared to take.

Statistically, most people are able to recall an experienced wrong - even a good-sized one - that has been forgiven with time. Hence, the decision to forgive is more common than it is rare. The journey to forgiveness is a process, one that is motivated by the desire to repair the relationship and reconnect with the transgressing party. This desire to maintain a connection with the transgressor serves to distinguish forgiveness from both reconciliation and forgetting. Our themes further indicate that forgiveness is a changed-nature event, in which people actively rework negative emotional responses to the transgression and transgressor.

These experiences suggest that forgiveness is motivated by the desire to maintain social bonds, and that some people will develop this desire to the point that it motivates the transformation of their previously negative emotional responses.

Empathy and Understanding in Forgiveness

Let me offer one thought on the process of forgiveness based on our own experience. This thought that I share is not scientific nor statistically driven by any means. However, it is a personal experience and conclusion from our own acts of forgiveness that has helped us through some of the darkest times of our lives. Quite simply, sometimes you can have more understanding and empathy for someone dear or near if you focus on what you might have done differently in the same situation. The thought and process of empathy and understanding are often tossed aside as part of personal reflection of what you would do should this challenging and painful act of betrayal, hurt, or mistake befall you or your relationship.

You don't need to be spineless. Forgiveness is not the act of admitting defeat or becoming demoralised such that your learned forgiveness does not result in a stronger sense of self in the end. Through forgiveness, you can still commit to the same values and principles and convictions you held before your experience of hurt without feeling compromised. In fact, forgiving someone and being willing to move forward can be empowering and a beautiful renewal of our core beliefs and values such that you can find something inside that you never thought possible of finding.

How My Journey Can Inspire Others

I am sharing my journey with you so it can inspire you. I spent almost two years of my life wanting to understand "my terrible situation." I couldn't think of it any other way. What was happening to me took on so many different forms. From my work situation to family strife. But after being knowing for a whole year things were wrong, and wanting so hard to put some kind of shape to the black hole I couldn't stay in. What I discovered not only was able to change my life in remarkable ways, but absolutely every aspect in every person's life who was involved. The two main characters in my situation. I came to understand, weren't really doing anything out of the ordinary. I was the one with the problem. My beliefs, opinions and present conditions were all interwoven into each other and based on a system of "society." They were victims, as I had been.

Their actions were not truly as they intended, but because they suffered from the role, I had constructed for them. Also, I could forgive these characters and see them as who they truly were - just a person single focused on their desire out of life. With sincere heart I can wish them peace.

Sharing Vulnerability and Strength

I believe that the bond of trust and identification that comes from sharing vulnerability is essential in helping another person learn about our own experiences. For many, sharing the pain of their journey offers strength to those on similar journeys. Social workers, chaplains, and spiritual care providers seem to be effective in facilitating forgiveness programs. Indeed, another study which addressed a broader array of mental, physical, and spiritual health  measures found pastoral counselling to be an effective intervention in improving anger, hope, and overall spiritual well- being among individuals with chronic disease. Furthermore, more diverse member networks might allow participants to feel less isolated after sharing their experiences, to learn from a greater diversity of participants, and to provide a broader network of support for the challenging journey toward forgiveness. A study directed to family caregivers had similar findings. Based on the belief that personal stories of tough love in professional and personal relationships among 12 nurse educators would showcase how difficulties in relationships resulted in healing, joy, and wisdom, researchers applied a Heideggerian nursing theoretical description with the aim of understanding the significance and essence of shared life experiences within relationships. Findings included the valuing of vulnerability and being in the moment as essential to relationships and teaching, and moral implications and responsibilities of connections.

Conclusion

I have learned important lessons from personal stories on forgiveness. People who are willing and able to forgive have learned to cope with life's quandaries by relying on their own experiences. They are not necessarily quick to forgive, nor are they unaware of the barriers to forgiveness. They are not amnesiacs, nor are they in denial about the need to recognise aggression, hold people accountable for their actions, or remove themselves from abusive or life-threatening situations. They are people who have chosen to work through the pain, to be transformed in the process, and to come out whole on the other side.

We learn beautiful lessons of courage, tenacity, and spirituality in hearing and absorbing the life stories that forgiveness signifies. In my own life, I have learned to try to develop those characteristics through my own efforts at forgiveness. In the strict sense of the term, I forgive a little at a time. Hesitantly, I take steps on a long, slowly progressing trajectory. Initial steps are often feigned or requested. If those introduction stages go well, movement forward increases my equanimity and hope, for perpetuation means passage downstream various obstacles on my road to a happier life. From hurt, to hope, to healing, and then to wholeness and history. I have learned that one can survive the grieving, achieve transcendent hope, and be transformed through the repetition of painful and trying efforts of forgiveness. And that is when people really begin to prepare the written record of their life stories.

I found immense diversity in people's approaches to cultivating forgiveness. Some advice: try a variety of techniques. Everyone's journey to forgiveness will be unique. What works for one person may not for another. Therefore, experiment with different paths—engaging in art, writing, music, or finding inspirational quotes. Even trying out yoga and exercise—not typically considered mediums for achieving forgiveness—may help. Pick a time that works for you. As the results indicate, it does not matter when you decide to work on cultivating forgiveness. Apply specific techniques over time. Repeated exposure to these techniques could increase their effects.

Use your spirituality. Given forgiveness's spiritual underpinnings, drawing on spiritual teachings or practices may help you on your journey to forgiveness. Try experiencing forgiveness through acts of kindness or prayer, creating a spiritual environment by incorporating elements such as forgiveness, reflection, or meditation into your life.

Be patient and don't give up. Those who continue to apply forgiveness strategies may be more likely to succeed. Times may vary for different transgressions, so that results may come about at different rates. Proceed at the pace that is comfortable for you to receive the maximum benefit. In addition to following these practices, you might consider asking yourself self-reflective questions such as the following: What emotions can forgiveness evoke? Can negative experiences lead to resilience? Can forgiveness foster optimism about the world?

About the Author:

Dr. G.A. Asif Jamal, M.Sc., M.Phil., Ph.D., FNSF, is an Associate Professor in the Department of Botany at Justice Basheer Ahmed Sayeed College for Women (Autonomous), Chennai, Tamil Nadu, India. With 20 years of teaching experience, she is a Guinness World Record holder for contributing to the world's thickest book. Dr. Jamal is also an ISO Internal Auditor, IPR specialist, and Certificate Course Coordinator. She has completed various certificate courses in health, plant physiology, and biotechnology. An Environment Management and Energy Audit Lead Auditor, she holds five collaborative patents, has authored six books, published ten research papers, and guided nine undergraduate projects. Dr. Jamal has presented numerous research papers internationally, earning multiple awards and honours.

CHAPTER 18

How infertility led to my greatest

BLESSING

Tami D. Garcia

At midnight, on the dot, I woke up and looked to my right at my mother. I said, "Hi, mommy, I'm going home today." This moment, on the thirteenth day of my hospitalisation, marked the beginning of my journey toward forgiveness – a path I never expected I would be on. Reflecting on this moment, I realise it was the first step in reclaiming my life.

But let me take you back to where it all began...

I grew up in a loving Caribbean family, surrounded by the warmth and wisdom of my grandmother and aunts. For the first ten years of my life, I was an only child, niece, and grandchild, experiencing both the joys of undivided attention and the loneliness that comes with it. My father was largely absent, a void that also shaped my understanding of family and my dreams for the future.

Our home was filled with beautiful stories of immigration, the islands, Caribbean food, music, and laughter. My great-grandmother and grandmother were pillars of strength and taught me the value of perseverance and resilience. My aunts showed me different facets of womanhood and motherhood. My mother showed me unconditional love.

I knew I wanted a house full of children from an early age. I dreamed of creating the big family I didn't have growing up. This desire was a driving force in my life, shaping my decisions and aspirations. I tried to do the right things to prepare for a family of my own. However, I quickly learned that even with preparation, not all things are of my making, and flexibility, understanding, and forgiveness would be essential life skills.

In my twenties, I learnt I had fibroids. It was a shock, but I remained optimistic. In 1998, I received an additional diagnosis of ovarian cysts, but still, I didn't let that get me down. By 2003, however, things took a severe turn with an additional diagnosis of stage 4 endometriosis. The news was shocking, and I was prepared to do whatever it took to be healthy and become a mother.

This final diagnosis led to surgery to remove as much of the problematic tissue as possible. I remember waking up from the anaesthesia, groggy and disoriented, to find my mother holding my hand. Wherever I was, if I needed her, she was there. The road to recovery was tough, both physically and emotionally. Each day brought new challenges – managing pain, dealing with hormonal fluctuations, additional medical treatments, and facing the uncertainty of my reproductive future. But I held onto hope, believing this was just a temporary setback on my journey to motherhood.

Then came the conversation that would change everything. My doctor, a kind woman with empathetic eyes, sat me down for a serious talk. She wanted to know if I still wanted children. Of course, I did. My desire for a family hadn't wavered. But then came the blow – she told me that due to all the challenges I have with the fibroids, ovarian cysts, and endometriosis, it had taken over. I had very little space to maintain a healthy pregnancy, so I had one year to get pregnant. I wasn't married yet, barely into my early thirties, and suddenly faced with a ticking biological clock that seemed to be racing faster than I could keep up. The pressure was immense. How was I supposed to find a partner, fall in love, and conceive a child all within a year? It felt like an impossible task.

Determined to take control of my fertility, I dove into research. I spoke with several fertility specialists, each consultation filling me with a mixture of hope and anxiety. After careful consideration, I chose Shady Grove Fertility in the Washington, DC, metro area. Their reputation was stellar, and they offered a program that felt like a safety net – for $25,000 plus medication costs, I would have multiple attempts to get pregnant. The financial burden was heavy, but the emotional stakes were even higher.

But there was still one glaring issue—I was single. The reality of pursuing single parenthood hit me hard. It wasn't the family story I had imagined for myself. I spent many days and nights crying into my pillow, doubtful and afraid. Was I ready to do this alone? Could I be a mother and raise my child without a father? I was a product of a single mother. However, I wanted different, but it seemed this was my fate. I had to accept this to move forward.

In a moment of what I can only describe as desperation, I did what many people seriously trying to have a baby alone would do: I asked a few friends if they wanted to be my baby daddy. Pretty funny, right? "Wanna go half on a baby with me?" I'd joke, masking my fear with laughter. It seemed like a joke, but I was dead serious. Unfortunately, there were no takers!

Realising I was indeed on this journey alone, I took the next step—choosing a sperm donor. It was a surreal experience. Over the next few days, I got together with a few friends at home and over the phone. For something that was such a life-altering decision, my good friends, both near and far, made it a fun experience.

I started with three failed Intrauterine Inseminations (IUI), a procedure where sperm is placed directly into the uterus during ovulation. When these attempts were unsuccessful, I moved on to In Vitro Fertilisation (IVF), a more complex process where eggs are fertilised outside the body and then implanted in the uterus. My IVF journey was brief but intensely impactful. It was a rollercoaster of hope and disappointment. Daily injections accompanied by a prayer for success became a ritual. The first IVF attempt failed, leaving me devastated, but I was ready for try #2. Each failure felt like a personal blow, but I remained hopeful that my perseverance would eventually be rewarded.

The second attempt was different. Not only did it fail, but I also started feeling unwell with persistent pain and a general sense of feeling all around terrible. I called and visited the doctor's office multiple times, trying to convey that something wasn't right. However, my concerns were dismissed and attributed to an emotional woman who had another failed IVF cycle. I felt unheard and invalidated; my concerns were brushed aside.

"This is just what happens sometimes. You are overreacting. It's all in your head." they'd say, their words did little to ease my growing anxiety and pain. "No, we don't need any additional tests, there's no need. No, we don't need to look at you; you are ok." Looking back, I can't be sure, but I feel confident saying that unconscious (and maybe some were conscious) biases played a role in how my concerns and complaints were received.

As I struggled with my health concerns and being ignored, I couldn't help but wonder if my experience as an Afro-Latina woman was playing a role. It wasn't just about me anymore; I began to see my story as part of a larger, troubling pattern. I learned that women of colour often face similar struggles in healthcare settings, with their pain and symptoms frequently downplayed or ignored. This disparity can lead to delayed diagnoses and inadequate care, sometimes with devastating consequences. My journey through infertility and near-fatal illness wasn't just a personal battle; it was a stark reminder of the urgent need for change in how our healthcare system treats women of colour.

Little did I know, my experience was about to become even more harrowing, bringing these systemic issues into sharp focus. About a month after my second failed IVF, at 3 am on December 27, 2005, I woke up screaming in the worst pain I had ever felt. It was unbearable, and I felt like my body was at war with itself. I called my best friend, Ariana, who lived just five minutes away. Without hesitation, she rushed over to take me to the ER. We waited for what felt like an eternity. When I was finally seen, they couldn't determine what was wrong. They gave me pain medicine and sent me home, telling me to follow up with my doctor. The dismissal felt like a physical blow, compounding my pain with frustration and fear. Again, I could not understand how they did not see anything concerning because my pain was real.

Knowing something was seriously wrong, I contacted my regular gynaecologist. Her response was immediate and decisive. Within seconds of examining me, she said, "I don't know what's wrong, but you need to be admitted to the hospital right now."

The next few hours and days were a whirlwind and mostly a blur. Doctors and nurses rushed in and out of my room. Their urgent whispers and concerned glances told me more than their words did. And even if they said anything to me, I could not remember or was of the right mind to answer. I felt like I was watching a medical drama unfold, except I was the patient fighting for her life. Thankfully, my mother was on the next plane from Cleveland, Ohio, to Washington, DC, a few hours after I was admitted to the hospital. My mother was amasing; she stayed with me for 24 hours a day. She was the advocate I needed.

The diagnosis, when it came, was shocking. I had sepsis, a life-threatening infection that had spread throughout my body. The next few weeks would become a blur of surgeries, procedures, and a fight for survival. Little did I know that this harrowing experience would not only change my body but also alter the course of my entire life. The first surgery they attempted was cancelled because they were not prepared for what was happening to my body; my insides were liquefying. The doctors were astonished I wasn't already dead or in a coma.

"Didn't your doctors know you were sick?" they asked repeatedly in shocking disbelief. They also said that if I had not come in when I did, I would have been dead within 24 hours.

What followed was a series of emergency procedures, including two blood transfusions, an appendectomy, the removal of part of my bowel, and a complete hysterectomy. My body, which I had hoped would nurture new life, was now being cut apart to save my own. I remember the doctor asking me if I understood that the procedure I was going to have would leave me unable to have children. With tears in my eyes, I looked at my mother, who also had massive concern in her eyes, as I said yes. It was a heart-wrenching moment, accepting that my dream of biological motherhood was over.

During my time in the hospital, I moved between life and death. With each day I stayed, the likelihood of my going home was lower. I hated being there. I hated the smell of the hospital, the taste of the food when I ate, and the bathrooms. I remember how they never seemed clean to me. The irony is that a hospital should be the cleanest place you go. Yet it is where other diseases are picked up if you stay long enough.

Day 13 was the worst. The doctors told my mother there was nothing more they could do. A pastor was called. I slept all day, only waking to vomit. Then, at midnight, something shifted, and a strange peace settled over me. I woke up, looked at my mother, and said, "Hi, mommy. I'm going home today." I immediately got out of bed after being in for 13 days and started walking the halls. The nurses clapped. No one thought I was going to make it out of the hospital. They all said it was a miracle. I said…but God.

The aftermath of this seemed just as devastating.

Not only had I lost my ability to have children, but I also lost my job. I plunged into a deep depression. The weight of these losses felt suffocating. I didn't understand what I had done to deserve all of this. Most people didn't understand what I had been through. Their well-meaning but misguided attempts at comfort often felt like salt in my wounds. "Kids are more trouble than they are worth anyway." You can have mine, trying to make a joke. Or you can always adopt," they'd say, as if it were a simple switch to flip. Someone I had once cared deeply for even told me to "get over it," but his words hurt the most. Then there were the people who never called or stopped by at all.

I was angry and felt cheated out of a literal and figurative life. I was furious at the doctors who had dismissed my concerns, at my body for failing me, and at my ex-supervisor for firing me.

I was angry at the unfairness of it all. Anger became my constant companion, and I knew something needed to change for me to get back to life. I didn't want it to be forgiveness because I didn't feel those people were worth it. But in the end, I was only hurting myself.

This was my first step towards forgiveness, acknowledging that holding onto this anger hurt me more than anyone else. At first, forgiveness felt like surrender—why should I let go? But as I held onto that anger, I realised it was holding me back from healing.

Forgiveness didn't come quickly. It was a daily choice, a constant battle against bitterness and resentment. I started with small steps – acknowledging my pain without letting it consume me. I learned to separate the actions of those who failed me from my worth and my future. Each day, I chose to release some of the anger, understanding that forgiveness was for my healing, not theirs.

My aunt Nickie, who had both adopted and biological children, became a lifeline. Our conversations were filled with laughter and hope amid darkness.

When I asked her how I would know if I could love adopted children as much as I would my biological ones, her response was simple yet profound: "You will never have biological children, so all you will do is love your child. There is no difference. You will love them, and your child will love you."

Those words were what I needed to hear. They opened a new possibility, a different path to motherhood that I hadn't fully considered before. It was then that I realised that I was ready to move forward. I had to let go of the life I imagined and embrace the one meant for me.

The decision to adopt was both terrifying and exhilarating. Each step of the process was filled with a mixture of hope and fear. Would I be a good enough parent? How could I afford it? The paperwork, home studies, and waiting felt endless. But with each step, I felt more confident that this was the path I was meant to follow.

Now, as a mom to a beautiful, intelligent, hilarious, and feisty 13-year-old, I can't imagine loving anyone more. The sound of her laughter, the warmth of her hugs, and the fierce light in her eyes when she's determined are the things that now define my life. My daughter, with her Ethiopian heritage, has opened a whole new world to me. Her presence in my life has been the greatest blessing, transforming my pain into a profound love and purpose.

My experience of disconnection—from my cultural heritage, fertility, health, and nearly my life—sparked a deep desire to help others connect. As I had to reconnect with my body and spirit through forgiveness, I realised the power of reconnecting people with their cultural heritage. This became my mission, transforming my pain into a purpose larger than myself.

I started a company dedicated to helping people reconnect with their cultural heritage and identity. This work has been deeply fulfilling, allowing me to touch lives in ways I never imagined. I've become an author, advocate, and storyteller and begun building an ecosystem around cultural heritage and identity. Through this work, I've come to firmly believe and advocate a core principle: Your cultural heritage is yours, no matter how little or how much you know, how large or small your DNA percentage. It's your birthright, your story, and no one can take it from you.

My mindset before and after my near-death infertility ordeal is different. Right after the incident, I was consumed by unfairness and anger. The constant migraines, the tightness in my chest, the shallow breaths – they were physical manifestations of my emotional turmoil. After acceptance and forgiveness, I found a deeper understanding of my strength, resilience, and purpose. I realised that while the medical system needs 

reform, my ability to forgive was essential for my healing. This process seeped into every aspect of my life, softening my interactions with others and allowing me to approach challenges with more compassion and understanding.

Forgiveness became less about excusing others and more about freeing myself. I learned that forgiveness was not a one-time event but a continuous process, a daily choice to let go and move forward.

Today, as I watch my daughter grow and thrive and as I work to help others reconnect with their cultural heritage, I am reminded of the transformative power of forgiveness. My journey has taught me that forgiveness is not a single act but a continuous process. It's about choosing, day after day, to let go of bitterness and embrace hope. It's about finding the strength to turn pain into purpose and setbacks into stepping stones. And finally, it is not a sign of weakness but the ultimate act of strength and self-love.

To those navigating forgiveness challenges, remember: Your journey is yours. There's no timeline, no right or wrong way to forgive. But in choosing to forgive, you choose freedom. You write your own story, which isn't defined by what happened to you but by how you chose to rise above it. This is the true power of forgiveness—it doesn't just provide healing; it opens doors to a future filled with possibility, love, and unexpected blessings. Practical steps like journaling, meditation, and seeking therapy can aid in this journey, helping you to process and let go of the pain.

I never thought that I would survive infertility, but now I am grateful for the gift it ultimately brought me. I am thankful for being my daughter, Isley Rahwa's mother. I could not imagine my life any other way. My journey of forgiveness has led me to this place of gratitude and joy. So, for this unfortunate and unexpected experience of infertility, I thank you and am grateful. Infertility brought me to my daughter, and through her, I have found a new purpose and joy in life.

About the Author:

Tami D. Garcia is an author, cultural heritage reconnection coach, and advocate for global understanding. Raised disconnected from her cultural heritage, Tami's journey of self-discovery ignited her passion for helping others embrace their roots. As the founder of Routes 4 Roots and author of the Amazon best-seller "Rediscovering Your Roots," she empowers individuals to find belonging and confidence. Currently world-schooling with her Ethiopian daughter in Mexico, Tami continues to break down barriers and foster acceptance across diverse audiences. Her work spans cultural integration, AI consulting, and storytelling, all aimed at creating more inclusive environments. Tami's transformation from disconnection to empowerment fuels her mission to help others heal, grow, and fully love all aspects of their identity. Drawing on 30 years of experience across diverse sectors, she tackles societal challenges effectively. Tami's life experiences—including infertility, adoption, solo parenting, and caregiving—have deepened her empathy and resilience. For more information, visit tamigarcia.com.

CHAPTER 19

Go back to move FORWARD

Aretha Naomi Taylor

It was 2015, two years after moving from Brooklyn, New York to Port Saint Lucie, Florida where I was staying with my mother to be her part time care giver. On this particular morning, I noticed that my mum was being short with her aid, for no reason so I asked her what was wrong, but she never answered me. I was trying to figure out what had happened that morning, to put her in such a rude mood, considering we had had a great time the night before with my sister Marva, who had spent the night. Again, she snapped at the aid, so I asked "mum what is wrong with you? Why are you being so rude?" She then replied, "she works for me, not for you so this has nothing to do with you". "So, does that give you the right to speak to her disrespectfully? This is someone who's caring for you and you're treating her like this?" "How am I treating her?" she asked. "Why don't you mind your business? Who are you to defend her?". "Mum you really need to learn how to speak to people. You've been moody all morning and you're taking it out on everyone." She didn't like that I was defending the aid and that I was correcting her behaviour, so she got angrier and began to shout at me. My sister was sitting in the family room watching TV, and was telling me to just ignore her, but I didn't want to ignore her. We've been ignoring her behaviour far too long and did not stand up enough for ourselves or for each other, so I began to get angry, and said "mum you are a bully and a war monger. You need to look at yourself and check your attitude and the way your treat others" "How do I treat other's?" "What have I ever done to you" she asked. And just like that...When she asked that question it triggered something inside of me that had been lying dormant since I was 13 years old and all my pain and anger came gushing out, and I erupted like a volcano.

"What have you ever done to me you ask? I'll tell you what you did to me. When I told you that your boyfriend was having sex with me, you reluctantly asked him to leave and then you took him back two weeks later. You had the nerves to knock on the bathroom door and gave me some ridiculous speech that you were taking him back because you needed the financial help. You were my mother. You were supposed to protect me, but instead you made this man come back to continue to rape me. You put money before your own daughter. You never asked me how I felt. I didn't have a voice. My feelings didn't matter. You gave him permission to rape me mom, that is what you did to me, and you have the audacity to sit there and act as if you were the perfect mother." By this time, I was hysterically crying, trembling and very emotional. I needed my mother to hug me and tell me how sorry she was and that she loved me, but instead, my mother called me a lying good for nothing bitch. My sister instantly came to my defence and had to remind my mother that it was her who made that phone call to her at work to let her know what her boyfriend was doing to me and that it was her who forced my mother to put him out. To our disbelief, my mother called us both liars and told us to get out of her house. I couldn't believe my mother's reaction and that I was going through this again. When I told her that it stopped only because I told my brother Gee, who had had an altercation with the man and threatened him, she didn't believe me, so she called him to ask if it were true. I couldn't believe my mother still didn't believe me after all these years. She was in complete denial of her part in it. She called me all sorts of names that day. I felt betrayed once again by her and violated, so I packed my things and my sister, and I left her house.

On our drive to my sister's house, I cried in the car, as my sister tried to console me. I was devastated, hurt, disappointed and angry. I wound up leaving Port Saint Lucie two days later. I didn't want to be there. I didn't want to be around my family, I wanted to be with friends, so I took a bus to Fort Lauderdale to spend some time with my friends. I cried all the way on the bus ride, which was three hours long. I didn't care if anyone saw me crying. This was how I was feeling, and this was what was needed. I couldn't stop the tears even if I wanted to. These were tears that were bottled up for years and needed to pour out. Tears that were buried deep that needed to be Dugged up. Tears of feeling lonely, and afraid, tears of feeling un-loved by my own mother. Tears of sadness, depression and anger, tears of betrayal. I cried every day for one week, but I realised that it wasn't the 47-year-old woman who was crying, but it was that 13-year-old girl, whose voice was taken from her, who wasn't allowed to cry or show her emotions. Who felt rejected and was constantly put down by her mother. That 13-year-old who didn't love herself then, because no one told her she could. That 13-year-old who felt defenceless and who wanted to be heard, who wanted to be comforted by the arms of her mother, that's who was crying. I needed to go through this process, no matter how long it would take or what the process looked like. I needed this for myself. This was a time to heal from those deep wounds and from that trauma. I needed to heal from shame and guilt. The guilt that I felt from not fighting back, and not telling sooner.

I had to now deal with my feelings and to know them and understand them. I had to resolve them. Feelings that I had internalised for so long, because I was taught to do that back then. What was that process like? It was painful, because I literally had to go back to that time in my mind and allow myself to go through the emotions. Sometimes we MUST go back, to move forward. My "eruption" was because I never dealt with my emotions, so I needed to sit with my emotions for a while and process them all. I did a lot of talking with myself and much praying, and that's when I realised that I hadn't forgiven my mother and that I hadn't forgiven the man who abused me. This man who had been dead for years, I was still carrying anger and unforgiveness for him. Unforgiveness is like a disease; it spreads. It affects you mentally, emotionally, spiritually, physically and those around you. It affects your relationships, your household, your behaviour and the choices you make. unforgiveness makes you and your environment unhealthy. I did not want this for myself. I did not want to nurture my hurt and anger. I wanted and needed to FREE myself of them, and I never again wanted to behave like that toward my mother, so I had to make the choice to forgive her, the abuser and myself. "For if you forgive others their trespasses, your heavenly Father will also forgive you. But if you do not forgive others, then your Father will not forgive your trespasses." (Matthew 6:14-15)

I had allowed two months to go by before calling my mother. When I finally did, the phone call went something like this..." Hi mum" "Hello Rita". "How are you?" I asked. She replied and said, "I am doing well" "How are you doing?" she asked. "I am well mum". "Did you have breakfast yet?" I asked. "Not yet, but I had my tea already for the morning." "Is the aid there yet "? "Yes, she's in the kitchen making my breakfast" she said. "Okay mum, I'm gonna let you go get ready for your breakfast. I was just giving you a quick call to say hello and to let you know that I'll be there soon to see you" I heard her voice break up when she said "okay, I'll see you soon" We then said good-bye.

Shortly after that call, I bought my greyhound bus ticket to Port Saint Lucie. I didn't tell my mother that I was coming to see her. I was going back as a different person. I was going back as a healed person from that hurt and trauma, and she needed to see that I had forgiven her. When I walked into the house my other sister Yvonne and the aid were there. I greeted and chatted with them for a while, before I headed to my mother's room where she sat in her favourite chair listening to the Jimmy Swaggart Channel. She was partly blind, so she didn't see me walk into her room, but she knew our voices, so when I said, "Hi mum" she recognised it was me and said, "Hello Rita" and burst into tears. I bent down and hugged my mother and kissed her on top of her head while she wept in my arms like a child. Her mouth never said the words "I am sorry", but her tears said it all.

That was a very rare moment for both of us, because growing up, my mother never displayed affection. She didn't hug us, she never said she loved us, and she never kissed us. My mother had her own issues that she never dealt with, and I saw what it did to her and to the family. She raised eight children by herself with very little to no education and skills. Raising children in Jamaica where we were born was extremely hard on her. She went through a lot of traumas, struggles and heartaches in her days. My mother was 89 years old during this time, so she was pretty much set in her ways. She too was carrying a lot of anger, hurt and unforgiveness from her past and it showed in her life, her behaviour her attitude, her choices and her mental and emotional state.

My mother was verbally, emotionally, physically, and mentally abusive. She had eight children, 40+ grandchildren, 20+ great grand and about 2 great, great grand, yet she was alone. Her house was empty. No one wanted to be around her, because of her mental and emotional condition caused by what she was holding on to. I wanted to point this out to her, but she was very difficult to deal with and to talk with, so I needed to be strategic in my thinking and my ways of approaching her. My mum had bipolar disorder all our lives, but we didn't know it. She herself didn't know it. We found out when she was 91 years old. We didn't even know what Bipolar was growing up, we just knew something was wrong and that her behaviour wasn't normal, but that was our "normal".

She caused so much strife and division in the family that most of us till this day don't have a relationship with each other. She behaved the same way in her church, with her neighbours and with all the aids who cared for her.
They would all quit after being with her for only a few weeks or a couple of months at the most. She had no friends, and no visitors, because she pushed everyone away.
This is the disease of un-forgiveness that I mentioned. Do you see how it spreads and affects everything and those all around you?
My mother suffered from Chronic depression caused by trauma. She too experienced rape, betrayal, abandonment, physical abuse and so much more, but she didn't know how to let go of the hurt,

pain, anger and the unforgiveness. I wanted my mother to be free, but I don't believe she realised that she was in BONDAGE.

Forgiveness is a process, but you must be willing to go through the process. Many people believe that forgiveness means to allow the person back into your life to cause you to be hurt again, but that isn't the case. It's releasing the weight of the hurt and anger. It's about YOUR Healing. Forgiveness brings healing and freedom. Holding onto Unforgiveness can also cause you to have physical pain, ailments and sicknesses, including cancer, brain tumours, heart attacks and strokes. When you forgive, you live a healthier mental and emotional life, which affects and heals the other areas of your life. Mental Health is a huge topic now-a-days, especially after Covid, but what does mental health really look like? It's more than going to the spa or taking a vacation. It's more than removing toxic people from your life. Sometimes, YOU are the Toxic person.

I can attest to that, because I was once toxic and abusive. I was the problem in one of my past relationships. When I was twenty-two years old, I met a guy whom I was in a four-year relationship with. I verbally, mentally, physically, and emotionally abused him for four years. It wasn't until he said to me one day "if you do not change, you are going to be like your mother, old and alone" It shook me to the core and forced me to look at who I was and I didn't like what I saw. I didn't like who I was becoming to myself, my daughter and my relationship, so I had to make the strong decision to work hard at NOT becoming like her. I had no right getting into a relationship with someone during that time in my life, because I was so angry and hurt and I didn't know how to have a healthy intimate relationship with anyone including myself. I first needed to deal with me and my pain, but I didn't know any better. I broke this young man emotionally and mentally. Four years ago in 2020, I decided to call him and apologised and asked for his forgiveness.

For you to have a healthy mind, you must first be emotionally healthy. Your emotions affect you mentally. We must be willing to go to the root cause of the pain, face it and deal with it. We must be willing to go to the source of the pain and that's one of the main reasons why I needed to go back to my mom's, because she was the root cause of my pain going all the way back to the womb and I needed to face her.

I needed to have conversations with her that were hard and painful. I needed to understand her, and to know what some of the things were that she had endured, because then I could understand ME. This was generational, and I needed it to stop with me and not pass it onto my daughter. I saw that mental illness was in my family by speaking with family members. Some were struggling with depression, some had bipolar disorder, and there were some who had anger and rage, and that was my struggle, so I needed to find out where that was coming from.

When my mum spoke of certain events in her past, she would get so angry and would begin to cry. I would ask her "mum, have you forgiven them?" She would just sit quietly, but you could see that she's thinking about the question but wouldn't answer. But by asking her this question, it made her do some self-searching. Sometimes, I didn't like to bring up the past to her, because I saw how painful some of it was for her, but I knew she needed to talk about it. This was her therapy. One day without me having to ask her, she shared her story about her rape by three men who forced her in the bushes when she took a short cut. While she spoke, I could see and hear the hurt, the regret, the guilt, the shame within her. I watched my mum cry so bitterly, that I felt her very emotions, but I was afraid to ask her if she had forgiven them. I didn't talk, I just listened to her. It was something she needed to talk about, so I did not interrupt her, I just allowed her to be vulnerable and transparent. The only thing I remember saying to her when she was finished crying was, "mom, it wasn't your fault" indicating that she needed to forgive herself. Many of us struggle with this and some of us feel like we don't deserve to forgive ourselves, because we see this as a form of punishment that we feel we deserve.

There were some things that she used to say and do that triggered me at times and took me back to my childhood, and I would react. I lost my patience with her often, and even sometimes, I got upset with her, but nothing like before. One of my triggers was when she accused me of lying.

My mum also had dementia and that comes with paranoia and accusations. She thought everyone was stealing from her, not remembering where she hid her money. She even accused us of stealing furniture and her clothes. I thought to myself, "what the heck is going on"? This felt like another level of torture. This behaviour was all new for us. We had never gone through this before, and we were trying to figure it out day by day.

My mother offended me almost every day while I was staying with her, and each time that she offended me, I had to work on forgiving her by letting go of the offense. When we hold on to offense, hurt, anger and unforgiveness, we give these things power over us. They control our Emotions and our lives. They hinder us from growing and becoming our greatest potential. Unforgiveness also gives birth to bitterness. Have you ever been around someone who is bitter? That person is negative, unhappy and miserable. There is no joy in them and being around them make you feel unhappy. Bitterness corrupts, divides, and devastates. It damages and destroys. This is why you MUST forgive. Forgiveness is a deliberate decision to release.

Forgiveness is a TRANSFORMATIVE change. It's a reconstruction of who you used to be transforming you into who you are supposed to become. Meaning, you are making a TRANSITIONAL shift Mentally, Emotionally, and Spiritually every time you forgive. Remember what I said about the hinderances you cause to your own growth when you choose to NOT forgive? Well, this is what will take place in your life when you choose to forgive. It will not only transform you, but also those

around you, including your family, your children, your spouse, your friends, your workplace, your household, and your environment. Your change will change others. Your change can and will change situations and circumstances. I am a witness to that. I slowly began to see the change in my mother and in her home. Every time that I forgave her, it brought a change within me, and it affected her. When you forgive, it can change the trajectory of an entire generation. It can build relationships, communities and bring restoration. Forgiveness is more POWERFUL than we think it to be! Self-forgiveness teaches us how to Love and treat ourselves. So many of us don't know how to treat ourselves, because we have NOT forgiven ourselves, which causes us to NOT have a relationship with self. Not forgiving yourself can also make you self-abusive, become angry and bitter toward yourself, and become self-sabotage.   You can even become emotionally disconnected from yourself. What kind of relationship do you have with yourself? What kind of people do you attract to yourself?

There is purpose in forgiveness. There's hope, there's unity, there's development.

Forgiveness brings peace of mind. I didn't see any of this growing up in my household or in my family, because my mother did not forgive. She held onto unforgiveness until it affected not only her, but her entire family and her environment. It corrupted the family, our behaviour toward ourselves, and each other. There was no love toward each other, but instead division, jealousy, discord, malice and anger. As the patriarch of the family, it was her responsibility to make sure there was unity and Love, but my mother could NOT teach us these things, because she held onto anger, unforgiveness and pain.

The Book On Forgiveness

I once asked my mother if she Loved herself, she never answered that question, but did what she normally would do when she doesn't know how to answer my questions…She just kept quiet with her thoughts and her emotions. My mother did love her children, she just didn't know how to love us. I used to pray and ask God to allow me to experience the LOVE from my mother that I never had growing up, even if it's for a moment, and he answered me.

We were back in Jamaica January 2018, when she was in the hospital recovering from a leg amputation. My two brothers (Leroy and Gee) and myself went to visit her in the hospital. When we walked up to her bed, my eldest brother Leroy began to weep. It was hard seeing her like that. He leaned over and kissed her and cried on her shoulders. I remember my mother stroking his head and kissing him. My brother Gee just kind of stood there watching just as I did until it was his turn to greet his mother with a hug and a kiss as he held back his tears. Now it was my turn to greet my mother, and I did so as I've always done over the years with "Hi mum" … She replied with excitement in her voice "Hi Rita my daughter, come give me a kiss". It was like I needed to get to her in a hurry, but when I tried reaching down to kiss her, I couldn't, because the railings on the bed were too high, so my brother Gee had to lower them for me. When I finally reached down to hug my mother, she gave me such a hug that I had never ever experienced from her before. My mother kissed me for the first time in my adult life and stroked my face. That's when I saw her for the very first time. I saw that mother that I wanted and needed growing up. That tender, loving, caring, sincere, nurturing mother that I prayed for, even if it were just for that moment, but that was the best moment I had ever spent with her.

When we were leaving, and saying our good-bye's, I knew that would be my last time seeing my mother, so when she asked, "Rita when will I see you again?". I responded and said, "I don't know mom, but you will see me again one day". On January 31st, 2018, the day I flew back to Florida, my mother passed away at the age of 92. Although those last four and a half years that I lived with her were very hard and emotional, I have no regrets. I had the opportunity to get to know my mother, in such a way that no one else knew or understood her.

She shared stories of pain, sorrow and laughter with me. We spent a lot of time together lying in her bed talking, crying, praying and laughing. Oh boy did we laugh; she had a great laugh. These are my Greatest and fondest memories of her, and I am grateful for those last years with my mother. This is what FORGIVENESS is…

About the Author:

Aretha Taylor is the Founder, Chair, President, and CEO of New Beginnings Outreach Program for Women, Inc., a non-profit organisation , and the Owner and Founder of New Beginnings Life Empowerment, LLC, both based in Brooklyn, New York. As a visionary entrepreneur and transitional life strategist, Aretha excels as a speaker, orator, podcaster, facilitator, radio host, pastor, philanthropist, and mentor. Her multifaceted career is dedicated to empowering women and fostering personal growth and transformation, making her a prominent figure in her community and beyond.

CHAPTER 20

A personal JOURNEY of a renowned MEDIA personality

Surin Punam

Forgiveness is one of the most important and valuable teachings of the heroes, prophets, and teachers who walk among us. By forgiving as a primary act of power and love, they have been able to maintain that state of spiritual bliss that martial warriors find so difficult to attain even once. The Achilles heel of the hero ethos is that, in order to embody it, one has to keep killing people. And at some point, love has its limits. For most of us, these are moral and emotional truths that we have absolutely no problem relating to. We are not warriors. We want to be lovers, not fighters. So why is it so difficult to practice the art of forgiveness? To understand this, and to learn how to truly practice forgiveness in our lives, we have to go back to those who walked among and taught us. For in their minds, hearts, and spirits, things were very different.

I have a secret. I am a women who has struggled some with the concept of forgiveness. Not just in concept, but in practice. I had managed to make a personal philosophy that held redemption and understanding in some of its most basic parts, and yet rebuilding a bridge after a betrayal was almost impossible for me. I could not forgive. It was not so much that I did not want to, it was just that the betrayal, in my mind, was always too large to repair the violation created. This was an easy level of understanding to reach. After much working with myself, I had come to understand that some things could not be undone. The "crime" was too heinous, the damage to the family too unacceptable, and the potential negatives at times were simply too great. Building a bridge over something like this would always be far too difficult. From that point, my feelings would flip right back into my personal morality about forgiveness and what it would take to be a better person if I did forgive. For many years, this was the bottom line. And I was good with that.

Significance of Forgiveness in Personal Growth

The healing power of forgiveness: A personal journey of a renowned media personality by Eugenia R. Macías. An exploration of the therapeutic value of forgiveness, this book, based on the story of a well-known media personality, Sylvia Pérez Magallanes, reveals the personal discovery of forgiveness. From nurturing the pain and anger of abuse and an unhappy marriage in the mind and spirit to healing from the emotional and mental pain, to an active life of transformation, peace, and joy. Sylvia will share her experiences of healing through an understanding of psychiatric treatment, the importance of prayer, and the tools that helped her and can help fellow sufferers.

From nurturing the pain and anger in the mind and spirit to healing from the emotional and mental pain, and an active life of transformation, moving beyond resentment, peace, and joy. The value of cultivating the practice of forgiveness is highlighted with contributions from professionals in the fields of psychiatry, medicine, spirituality, religion, and theology

The Incident with Family

Vicki Yohe is a renowned Christian recording artist and musician who writes, arranges, and produces her own music. She has been a media personality since 1995, hosting and co-hosting Christian talk shows, and independently producing and hosting her own television programming. Over the years, her voice has reached

millions of households across the nation. The focus of all of Vicki's work is to share joy and inspire her audience to take pause, restoring dignity, strength, and perhaps a conservative view. She also shares personal stories, hoping her audience might find some benefit.

Vicki Yohe once had a very poignant experience with a family member. A number of years ago, someone in her family accused her of embezzling money from a business they both had shares in. This family member fabricated false accounting records with the intention of extorting money from her. The personal betrayal was unexpected and unprecedented. This situation is retold in a song on Vicki's latest release.

In the grand scheme of things, the amount of money lost to the fraud wasn't very important to Vicki's business or family, but the hurt and the blowback was, and became pervasive, affecting the family as a whole. Through intensive work investigating both bank and personal accounting records, the matter was eventually resolved. Hiding her pain from the public as much as was humanly possible, she was able to maintain her upright standing in her community and hopefully save her family business. Besides the personal hurt and trauma at a time when her beloved father was dying, the professional cost and time away produced an upsurge of pain and anguish. Notwithstanding hours of prayer and self-examination, to forgive the subject and self would have to be a multi-year effort for Vicki. For Vicki to work through this would take more emotional time and effort than anything else in her whole life, indeed, less time than it would take her to recover physically from a vehicular accident that year in which she had two consecutive head-on crashes.

The Book On Forgiveness

Lessons Learnt

I have learned that parenting and guiding your children, regardless of their age, is a lifelong responsibility. You don't tell them a fact one time and wave away further responsibilities. Every parent affects generations to come, directly and indirectly... Think about it. Can you remember what your great great grandmother did for a living, unless she was a very famous personality? And yet, possibly, her decisions directly affected your life. Now, I am not promoting matriarchal influence over the family. I am saying that every adult in a family can affect the others positively or negatively. Decide to affect your loved ones positively - that's love and caring!

No matter how "botched" we have made our life, no matter how many people we hurt or how deeply we are disappointed - by others, by life or by God - we are living and so, must keep on learning to make the best of it. We are responsible for our behaviours. All your ugly behaviours had their source in you only. You alone must uproot and exterminate them permanently or you will destroy yourself and everyone around you who love you as well. Force the truth about yourself to come out of hiding. The truth will set you free!

The Book On Forgiveness

Empathy and Compassion

During this period, I began to feel that in every act, in every situation, there is such a thing as silence. And I felt that I could practice, develop, and heighten silence. This, I believe, is both Emersonian and Zen, and may make for a fuller life than, in my usual seeking state, I knew existed. From the time of our misfortune, in that abyss of disconsolation or

depression which nevertheless was not, could hardly be, without its moments of blessedness, there were wonders. There was an unexpected outpouring of brotherhood and of people's feeling that they were bearers of divine grace, that they were instrumentalities of boundless sympathy and love.

After I managed to help myself, I suddenly found that I could help others. I've never helped anyone before. I never thought that focus, tremendous focus, and single-mindedness will come when the cause is difficult enough, and fields wide enough. I am, more than I ever knew, enveloped in an aura of compassion and concern. Some people who have had widely varied experiences have given me the gift of truly understanding me. My own discovery was here, truly unplanned and unintended. Yet, for me, it has importance. Very distinct and, so far, personal importance. A huge number of people, friends, other associates, and even strangers, fascinated me by what had been their constant variance from the coarse, the crude, the animalistic which exists in myself, and was now manifesting itself in the fullness with which news interest enveloped, submerging many other values of which I feel myself capable.

Encouraging Forgiveness in Others

One thing I frightened myself with, was discussing forgiveness. I can't help but accept that I am often listened to when I go public about something. And I can't help but fear that by freely expressing forgiveness, someone facing the pain of feeling wronged may be left with a guilt trip for not being capable of such a thing themselves.

To some extent, this is quite unavoidable because the truth is that it is mainly by people helping each other, talking things over, lending a sympathetic ear, and sharing similar experiences that any form of forgiveness might eventually spring up. In offering a plea for faith and fortitude and forbearance to others, do I not do them a disservice? Do I not raise false hopes, cruelly taking advantage of their generous spirits? Suppose they are not surrounded by the same sort of overwhelmingly helpful affection that I have received, especially in these last two weeks.

I am sure the answer to such fears is mainly yes. I feel that by laying bare my own difficulties in dealing with upsetting circumstances and by describing the hopes and possible aspirations I retain, even against all obstacles and opposition, I also help others. If forgiving people happens only after they have appreciated the desirability of such an attitude, the best I can do is give them a chance to form any judgment sometime later down the track. It is absolutely only one among various options, and the preferability of such compassionate reactions, in the vast majority of instances, is a most profound revelation awaiting anyone in search of a measure.

Conclusion

Forgiveness, in my experience, really is the only prison worth escaping from. It is the only psychological discipline that is a world unto itself, a perfect circle that creates healing in everyone it touches. Yes, it has been a long journey, filled with surprises and unexpected treasures. It has felt a lot like climbing a mountain. But I had reached the top with this book, and now I can look down and see my life spread out before me. I can see, at least in part, the shape and pattern of my journey and I am aware, in a way I've never been before, of the healing power of forgiveness in a life. Yes, I am a different person now, unburdened and lighter for having ventured there. And even when the pain comes back, the pain buried so deep within my unconscious that only echoes can be detected, I am not that pain.

Understanding and practicing forgiveness is not just some kind of altruistic, feel-good, or holy thing to do. It is about one's own healing and freedom. In the profound wisdom of the Sermon on the Mount, Jesus said, "Love your enemies and pray for those who persecute you so that you may be sons of your Father who is in heaven." The original Greek word for "sons" translates as 'to become' and 'saviour'. Thus, 'to become free to become saviours' like the Father, as it reads in the original Greek. This is the natural progression of practicing forgiveness in living the ultimate truth, the root of truth of our reunion with God in unconditional love. As we persistently forgive, we gradually free ourselves from the chains that bind us in fear, the creative power of the fearful ego to continue binding us and others through the mind's miscreation's. As we continue freeing ourselves by forgiving, we generate an aura of liberation so that others around us may also free themselves.

About the Author

Punam Surin is a renowned media personality with over thirty years of experience as a senior announcer, program presenter, anchor, and actor at All India Radio and Doordarshan. Joining All India Radio in 1990, she has contributed to numerous national channels of Prasar Bharati, supported by top-notch scriptwriters, researchers, visualisers, and technical experts. Prior to this, she was a science teacher at St. Mary English Medium School, Jamshedpur. Punam has interviewed VIPs across various fields and made notable contributions to the 2010 Commonwealth Games. She has also appeared in popular Hindi and Bengali TV serials and currently hosts the motivational radio program "Namaste Yuva."

CHAPTER 21

The strength of FORGIVING and SHOWING compassion

Roxanne Boodhoo

There is so much hurt and hate in this fast-paced, high-tech world we live in. We are continually bombarded with negative stories that spill hatred on strangers; people we've never met, and by whom we have never been wronged. It's become safer not to trust people. But why? Shouldn't compassion and tolerance rule our thoughts and our actions? We'd certainly prefer to be treated accordingly. Forgiveness is a personal message and may indeed seem tough for many. However, during the difficult process, there is much peace and understanding to be developed in both ourselves and those around us. Let me share my experience with you. I am neither an academic nor a counsellor. I offer my observations to you based on the fact that not only did forgiving the people who abused me heal the real me, it also allowed me to live beyond being a professional victim. In my heart, I finally can feel free.

Significance of Forgiveness in Life

Forgiveness is an attribute of strong people. Everyone likes to be adjusted, loving, and successful. All imperfections in another bring us to appreciate that person and like him or her better, once our own imperfections are seen and understood. But before we come to appreciate those things, sometimes we are uncomfortable or perplexed even by a lesser error, and therefore offend. Forgiving is an opportunity. It is the beginning of courage and strength. All strong people enjoy forgiving friend or foe, without judgement. Therefore, forgiving is justifiable, and becomes significant for the personal growth of every person. It offers a hopeful step to the development and the improvement of human relations in a disordered world. If anyone can govern himself and deal kindly with others, he does favour everyone. In our natural state, governed by a God-given conscience directing our thinking, we do earn approval, positive response, and genuine affection. We do this not only for ourselves, but also for the good of others.

There are subtleties of forgiveness and atonement not easy to express. One is that different occasions evoke different attitudes about forgiveness. There is forgive-and-forget and there is forgive; that means, do not show your resentment and do not refuse to trust in the future. It is as if my house caught on fire, and I had to go to every room and throw out to those helping me every article I cherished. Such is my need to unburden my soul. Unlike my search for strength, I must take the time and exhibit poor taste. For those who have no great cause in life are always poor. In despair they fall. People who know that satisfying life is working toward something worthwhile, filled with purpose, fun, and good work, can rejoice in breaking and fixing, in giving and forgiving. Unlike the poor, they know life is serious, not solemn. Only forgive. A person is not responsible for change in anyone else. People do not have to live morally, up to expectations. A person does not sin when he does not succeed in making others moral. Everyone is responsible for himself. No one should sinning, or of needing to forgive. No one needs to atone for his own sin. At the other extreme, taking responsibility for oneself is not giving in to selfishness without consideration for other people. Responsibility for oneself is gladly taking part in every opportunity to practice first forgiveness by equivocation. Equivocation means meeting ourselves, when we deceive others. None of us freely admit our weaknesses. But we all have an innate urge to seek spiritual fulfilment; and eventually to recognise the truth.

Personal Experience

When my friend was about 25 and still single, she broke off her engagement to a very dear young man. Before a year had passed, he married someone else (no, there hadn't been anyone else all along), and it wasn't long before they started their own family. From their first, they adopted a little girl of two or three, who had a badly disfigured hand. Susan. A sweet, loving child... the kind who makes a person want to be better for their sake. But in public, she avoided Susan's eyes - not because of the hand, but because of what the hand did to remind me, not every day but often, of the implications of my past relationship with her mother... On her 33rd birthday, a good friend took her out for dinner.

As they walked into the restaurant, she saw Susan, who was about seven then, for the first time in over four years. There was no patch that night. No reservations. No defensiveness on either side. My friend felt elated, confused, and puzzled afterwards... because she hadn't thought of her hand.

At work, it sometimes happens that someone tells me of the deep and abiding hurt another person has caused them. Always my instinctive response is, "Forgive!" Eventually, I learned to hold my tongue and keep my expressiveness in check. Because one doesn't think in absolutes anymore, having taken the easy way out and selectively avoiding contact. Nor expect to be judged by one's own standards. It's a brave act of exposure on the part of the one who would offer the encouragement to another. Now I've begun to come to a different kind of appreciation... that kind children seem to have when they see beyond the wrapping without reference to the disfigurement. Not everyone has something weighing heavily on their conscience or a visible token of a mistake. But everyone carries the fingerprint of a mistake in one form or another.

Specific Story or Moment

The start of my forgiveness journey began with a soul-searching conversation with a precious friend. I had expressed to her the hurt I had been working through for a few years, but actually it was much longer than that. She candidly yet gently asked me if I had forgiven the person. I was actually doing quite well with recognising the hurts and disappointments and even in the earnest quest to move forward. But no, I hadn't forgiven. In fact, if I was being honest with myself, I was still a little bitter. What an achingly sour appendage bitterness is to every happy thought, what a hopeless encumbrance! The moment I recognised it was as if a bell sounded, a gong reverberated, time for change!

With honesty and openness comes empathy, understanding, compassion, and forgiveness. I was transformed. Not for the first time of course, but the warmth of each experience is the same. It is in the process of offering these gifts of the heart that I am the prime beneficiary. In the giving, I learn to receive—fully, deeply, and completely. It is a lovely cycle. The trek is long and at times steep, but oh, from what heights we then can view the world. The process of forgiveness is laden with gifts—hope, peace, growth, love. The removing of the layers of hurt, guilt, malcontent. Relief, joy, admiration, delight. There is joy yet to come in the removal of layers: layers of privilege, egotism, thoughtlessness, pride, prejudice—all that can obstruct a soul. Unblock, unshackle, unburden.

Lessons Learned

After the betrayal, it didn't take me long to realise that I was embarking on a very important journey. I also realised, "You can choose to let go and free yourself of pain, anger, and bitterness. It is a conscious and intentional act." I set out on a mission to learn as much as I could about forgiveness. The journey has been long and difficult but very rewarding. Following are a few lessons I have learned along the way.

I have learned that moving to the point of forgiveness does not happen overnight. Acceptance and grief are the first steps. Definitions which include the concept of surrender and letting go do not consider a few important steps. Blaming, hating, and taking revenge masked intense feelings of hurt, pain, fear, and more.

Accepting the need for comfort and security takes place long before any feelings of hate or fear are released. Grieving must occur before true surrender takes place. Forgiveness includes in its definition the ideas of surrender, freedom, and preventing revenge. When I chose to forgive so that I  could lessen the intensity of the pain, open up the wisdom of forgiveness, experience peace, and live again, I was electing to empower myself. The most important work anyone can do in mastering the transition of betrayal to forgiveness is to give thought of gratitude for their wonderful moments of potential chaos and their inner power that let them choose to act first. The pain leads to the wisdom gained. This transition of betrayal to forgiveness does not happen by accident. It requires preparation, practice, and patience.

Reflections and Insights

As I reflect back on my own journey of forgiveness, I am inspired by a reaffirmed commitment to be even more mindful of the negative impact caused by holding on to bitterness. The silent torment held within the soul can unwittingly foster feelings of hostility, despair, and fear, which in turn can breed and promote continuous acts of anger, aggression, and hatred. If we could respond to our inner fears, concerns, and pain with understanding, generosity, kindness, and compassion, maybe our individual worlds would be a much happier and more forgiving place in

which to live. For me, forgiveness is key to lasting peace and happiness. I have come to the realisation that to answer needs or wrongs with patience and kindness is an integral value dear to my heart, for only in this way will I truly be able to foster self-growth and happiness.

Reflecting back, I recognise there have been many turning points along the journey, but for me, my defining moment, my epiphany, my perception shift occurred one September day in 2012 at Crossroads. It was evident to me that given the smallest window of opportunity, given hope, protection, and the willingness to be patient and kind, to trust, I glimpsed their burgeoning self-belief. For me, the experience was overwhelming - I silently cried my heart out. My heart ached as I came to tolerate my disassociation from the love of a family who had been lost to me for so many years. Despite the pain this entailed, it led to a silenced heart, abused by broken dreams, healing itself through learning that in forgiving we experience ourselves becoming freer, unencumbered, awakening us to our true potential, love, and happiness.

Conclusion

I am not in any way adept at forgiveness. But it is merely a mere thought, feeling, and value, for which I am now, like any avid farmer seeks every event of rain persists on barren land, for this part of my life has been and can be one of the most rewarding experiences of the positive healing I have encountered thus far. I believe that forgiveness is but a greatest strength which one can manifest when overcomes transgression. For me, the battle of forgiveness can be easily summarised with the words of Saint Augustine. "O True Lord, cleanse me and purify me, let me never have to feel bilious against my brother, who is but you yourself. I have found that when I have not forgiven, especially when I have been unable to forgive myself, I have indeed become ill, mentally, physically, and in every other sense. My personal experience has taught me time and time again many of the affirmations and slogans like "courage to change the things I can" or "admit to God, ourselves, another human being the exact nature of our wrongs" spoken within the rooms of recovery.

These words and phrases which the founders of most recovery programs have incorporated in their steps are a way of life. They are impeachable when they are used for their express design and their intended purpose. I have found when I do use them, I am able to grow and experience freedom from the anguish and harm that not forgiving and being unable to let go of my many negative feelings have kept me from. For those of us who feel the need to grasp harder onto the reins of the wrongs done against us, or the wrongs we have done, we can assure ourselves of a life of absolute misery. Then perhaps we shall discover that we were hugging the cactus and wondering why it hurt so much. May we have the fortitude to look beyond the hurt and to strive to steadily to work the soil, and very carefully pull the weeds, year after year, until that persistent bittersweet growth becomes weaker, and gradually disappears.

Advice to others

Move on to a healthy lifestyle, embrace change in your life. Many self-help books teach you how to do this. When negative changes happen, cry and appreciate the lesson. Inform yourself and learn from it. Give it as a gift, whether you are in the direction of healing and forgiveness that helps you to  strengthen and mentally grow from your painful experiences. Once the true value of freedom is realised, I trust that you will eventually be curious about this personal guide. I am very hopeful that, in due time, after continuously and finally praying for a spiritual life of peace, tranquillity, and mental health, yes, peace, tranquillity, and wishful spiritual long life will come your way. Please remember, forgiveness allows the opposite party to be free, too. Finding solace is all about health and happiness. During the journey of complete escrow, travel, and enjoy.

I have taken on many roles in my life. I have been an Emergency Response Specialist, counselling people through the toughest moments of their lives. I have been educated as a tutor, helping students make good decisions for their future. I am a teacher. I am a mother. I have seen and felt, as well as helped many people through some of the worst decisions someone could ever make. I have spent my life counselling many in public safety. Some of the decisions made under public safety affected me deeply before I even knew it. I create things as I am living, learning, and growing.

Sometimes what we need most is someone who knows what we have been through, can lend an ear, and help us close the book. I have been told that people trust me simply because of who I am and where I have been. After all of my years of walking with people, counselling them through the biggest moments of their lives, listening, advising, and planning with them, I was not looking for my own personal journey that had gone unnoticed for nearly my entire life.

About the Author:

Roxanne Boodhoo is an accomplished professional with a diverse and versatile background. Her extensive academic training has equipped her with a wide range of skills and knowledge, enabling her to excel in various roles. Roxanne is known for her strong work ethic, diligence, and commitment to undertaking any responsibilities assigned to her. She is deeply passionate about helping and supporting others, engaging in multiple volunteer activities and advocating for various causes. As an advocate and humanitarian, Roxanne is dedicated to making a positive impact, striving to uplift those around her and contribute meaningfully to her community and beyond.

CHAPTER 22

FORGIVENESS
truly heals

Jacqueline F. Render

The Storm Within

The echoes of my own voice bounced off the walls, each word sharp and cutting. "It's your fault we are here and it's your fault that we continue in this cycle. I am angry with you to a point where I just don't want to look at you anymore." The intensity of my anger was like a storm, but what I didn't realise was that these words, though directed outwardly, were actually aimed at myself. Each accusation was a dagger piercing my own heart, inflicting wounds that only forgiveness could heal.

In front of the mirror, I wasn't just confronting my reflection; I was confronting my deepest regrets and self-disappointments. This temporary moment would be embedded in me for some time. It would dictate my actions and reactions to all situations in my life from now on. It would not allow me to move forward into something better. It would have me trapped until I was willing to take control of the real problem—the real thing that was causing my soul to ache inconsolably.

The Power of Self-Forgiveness

Self-forgiveness is the most critical process of healing I have ever experienced. I was trapped in a vicious cycle, constantly berating myself for past mistakes, present missteps, and future fears. It felt like an endless loop of self-reproach. Yet, this torment led me on a transformative journey. The journey of self-forgiveness, one I will never regret.

Finding Support and Realisation

I embarked on this path by joining a support group for individuals entangled in negative relationships of any kind. This group guided me through the process of forgiving others and the negative impacts they had on my life. I forgave my parents, siblings, friends, and even co-workers. However, despite these efforts, a wave of lingering anger and frustration remained. It was something that continued to tug at me even with the work that I had been intentional about addressing head-on.

Discovering the Root of My Anger

I couldn't comprehend why I was still engulfed in anger and frustration. I had forgiven those who had wronged me; logically, I should have felt better. But I didn't. This unresolved anger led to rash decisions, caused me to distance myself from those who cared about me, and even affected my physical health—I ate more and slept less. It also affected my mental health. I felt stuck, unable to pinpoint the source of my anger. If I could just pinpoint this anger, I could move forward. To my surprise, the world shifted as the pandemic struck and the door to self-forgiveness was opened.

The Unexpected Gift of the Pandemic

The pandemic was harsh and devastating globally, yet it saved my life. Forced into isolation, I was compelled to confront myself. It became clear that the anger I felt was internal. It was the source of the pain that lingered despite the previous work I had done. Every strategy I had learned for forgiving others, I now had to apply to myself. Initially, my attempts at self-forgiveness were fraught with self-criticism.

I had to adjust the strategies to meet the needs of forgiving myself and not others. As I did this, I quickly realised that if I continued with resistance and self-criticism it would only hinder my progress. The corrections I made were to approach myself with compassion, and fully embrace the process. Once I did, there was no stopping me. I gained clarity, a sense of accomplishment, and an unprecedented level of self-love. Forgiveness opened doors to the boundless possibilities of life.

The corrections I made were to approach myself with compassion, and fully embrace the process. Once I did, there was no stopping me. I gained clarity, a sense of accomplishment, and an unprecedented level of self-love. Forgiveness opened doors to the boundless possibilities of life.

Components of Self-Forgiveness

When you think about self-forgiveness, the components involved in them are important. These components are responsibility, remorse, restoration, and renewal. Each of these components was key to helping me to achieve my own self-forgiveness.

<u>Responsibility</u>

As I began this process, I had to evaluate my role in this situation. Taking responsibility for my own actions and recognising the impact they had on me without rationalising them. When I would find myself rationalising them, I took a deep breath and said to myself, "These are just the facts, and this is how it impacted me. Accept it and let's not live there." There was a lot of self-talk that helped during this process.

<u>Remorse</u>

Next, I had to show remorse and genuine feelings of regret. This part of the process is essential. This emotional response indicates that one understands the gravity of their actions and the harm caused. During this remorse, I cried and maybe even yelled a bit more. The difference this time versus before the start of the process was that I was not angry or upset with myself. I knew that I was on a journey of self-forgiveness. Knowing what I was doing eased the anger but did not diminish the feelings.

<u>Restoration</u>

When it was time to make amends and seek to repair my personal damage, I was willing to do the work to prevent recurrence, give myself grace as needed, and love myself along the way.

Renewal

This self-given grace was the renewal I needed to let go of the negative self-image and guilt associated with past, present, and future mistakes. It required embracing a renewed sense of self-empowerment.

The Steps to Self-Forgiveness

Let me walk you through the process that allowed me to forgive myself and heal

Step 1: Self-Awareness and Self-Acknowledgment

The first step is cultivating self-awareness and self-acknowledgment. You must be brutally honest with yourself about where forgiveness is needed. Recognise and admit that forgiveness is necessary. If you're not willing to be honest with yourself, it defeats the purpose of even starting the process. At this stage in the game, you have to get very real with yourself.

Step 2: Acceptance and Correction

Accept that mistakes were made but understand that each mistake provides an opportunity to learn a lesson. From these lessons, you can build steps that keep you from making the same mistake. This would be considered your correction. It is critical to write all of this information together. You need to write the mistake, the lesson and the applied correction. You will then need to look at it and ask yourself two critical questions. 1. Can you learn from the mistake and implement the steps needed for correction? 2. Are you willing to grow from it and break the cycle of repeating the same errors all while still loving yourself?

Step 3: Implementation and Forgiveness

Now, it's time to implement the steps you developed for correction and your process of forgiveness.

Step 4: Reflection and Affirmation

Reflect on your actions, your plan, and your mistakes. Make adjustments if needed. The biggest part of this process is to write a note to yourself highlighting all the positive things you have accomplished and the growth you have achieved. End the note with a bold affirmation: "I forgive you and I love you." In doing this you are able to refer to these letters as needed. It is like having someone (which is you) remind you just how amazing you are.

Please note: Writing is a big part of this process that allows you to see it in black and white on paper from beginning to end. You can determine right at the start if you are going to be vested in the process of self-forgiveness. As you move through your journey you are able to make adjustments and modifications to the plan you wrote out. As you reach your goal you are able to look back and see the growth and success you have made along the way. Without writing through this process you continue to hold bits and pieces of unreal places in your head and your heart. You may not write but the level of self-forgiveness you achieve will amaze you along the way, so write it out.

The Impact of Self-Forgiveness

These were and are my actions to heal and achieve the feeling of peace and freedom from processing through self-forgiveness. Remember that forgiving yourself is critical in life. If you don't you will harbour resentment towards yourself and have feelings of anger and confusion. This can lead to being stuck in a cycle where you blame yourself for things and often don't trust others. It can even cause you to feel unworthy of forgiveness from yourself as well as others. This affects your mental and

physical health. However, the benefits of self-forgiveness are immense: it allows you to make mistakes without self-condemnation, grants you a new sense of freedom, and fosters self-trust, preventing self-sabotage.

You will learn to give yourself grace through this process of self-forgiveness. Self-forgiveness opens doors to the boundless possibilities of life.

Embracing the Journey

Forgiving yourself can be challenging. We often believe we should know better as we age, and admitting our mistakes can be painful. Yet, self-forgiveness illuminates the darkest corners of our lives and helps us grow beyond our expectations. If I can achieve this, so can you. It's time to grow and glow into your season.

About the Author:

Jacqueline Render is a passionate coach, teacher, and motivator dedicated to inspiring personal growth. She empowers individuals to achieve their full potential, drawing from her experiences as a mother, educator, and mentor. An avid traveller, Jacqueline gains fresh perspectives to enrich her coaching approach. She holds a Masters in the Art of Teaching from LeMoyne College in Syracuse, NY. Jacqueline is a certified Life and Business Coach & Master Trainer. She is endorsed by Georgia as a Coach, Teacher Support Coach, and in Reading and Positive Behaviour Interventions and Support. With her wealth of knowledge and natural ability to connect, Jacqueline helps clients overcome challenges and pursue their dreams.

CHAPTER 23

Release PAIN and embrace FREEDOM

Shalini Mittal

Forgiveness is a powerful and often overlooked tool for personal growth. Webster's New World Dictionary defines forgive as "to give up resentment against or the desire to punish; stop being angry with; pardon." This definition embodies the essence of forgiveness. It is important to note, however, that forgiving does not mean condoning. For the purposes of understanding forgiveness and making use of practical advice, it is useful to use the above definition in our analysis.

Almost all of us have experienced the pain and frustration of being hurt by someone in our lives. It may have been painful words or subsequent ridicule. It may have been a long-standing and painful rivalry that has pushed an assortment of buttons that cause pain. Or, it may have been a deliberate, physical act of aggression, like a push, shove, punch, or some form of harassment. Whatever the act of aggression or harassment may have been, we all understand hurt, pain, frustration, and anger. The ultimate decision of how to handle the anger and pain, though, is our cholce.

If we fail to understand that decision is ours, and ours alone, not only is our inner healing impeded, but the associated power becomes 'owned' or controlled by whoever committed the act of aggression. They, in effect, 'own' our inner emotions of resentment and hurt. When managed, what's worse is that we can expect reciprocal acts of violence long into the future - or at least for a period of time that will likely feel too long until the passage of time becomes ripe, and our psyches slip the ready grip of anger's siege. We want pain replaced by healing, anger's trigger detached, and either a neutral or a positive state restored. This is at the heart of our urge to not only forgive but 'wholly forgive'. Small wonder, then, when entire cultures have internalised a powerful contemporary or supernatural mechanism-based rule, or a legal ethos that can sanctify the replacement of neutrality over the power of anger, negative memory & feelings, and ultimately, conquered the seething arenas of hurt—often into a raging inferno.

Personal Experience

In all of these intervening years, I have learned so much more about myself and about the tormenting feelings that accompany the injured and dissenting, the primary source for feelings of great hatred and disgust. It's taken me almost a quarter of my life to come to understand it. However I could no longer blame those or any other assailants for my remaining suffering. It was through my use of self-hypnosis and meditation to banish the past that I eventually managed to overcome the extreme inner turmoil I was suffering.

In the years that have followed, I have managed to come to terms with the loss, and I have made a lot of friends and made a lot of positive progress in my life. In that respect, I am hugely grateful to all the people who have made such a significant contribution to my general welfare. Our decisions and our choices result in each of us losing or extending control over our own lives, and when we have to learn about the resultant new regulations that intention requires us to obey, we should look at them always with an open heart because usually we can get some good things from them if we do.

Forgiving Betrayal

I had always considered myself a forgiving person, one who knew my boundaries and was able to move on with little difficulty. However, in relationships, I became acquainted with a great force - one that taught the true meaning of forgiveness, taught me about the power behind forgiveness, and changed my life forever. It was a force I'd experienced but never fully realised I had the power to use to my advantage. This force served me on one of the darkest days of my destiny, pulling me into a baptism of air, an almost tangible invisible force that enfolded me in a manner of presence and hope. This force is forgiveness, and it changed my life.

Our relationship dominated my life. We'd shared fun, confidences, tenderness, anger, and exploitation. I was so deeply impressed into the labyrinth of our relationship that separation seemed akin to losing my identity, allowing myself to be on the brink of emotional bankruptcy.

Although each day brought a pittance of despair, I did not have the courage to face the inevitable - I could not extricate myself from my self-imposed state of discomfort and loss.

That final chapter in our relationship occurred quite suddenly and without the benefit of prior warning. The event pivoted my life, shifting it into another arena altogether. During the last part of our relationship, he fell deeply in love with someone else. They married in what seemed only a matter of short weeks. Unprepared, I faced the ultimate challenge: the betrayal of losing him to someone who could so swiftly take away all the beauty we had shared. As I sat in the echoing darkness, I felt the movement of the Earth, the presence of others in the house who silently acknowledged my suffering and offered the delicate comfort of silence.

Lessons Learned

The most important thing I have learned through this journey is the importance of forgiveness in my life, so I have made a firm decision to spend the rest of my living days in the pursuit of peace, joy, and tranquillity for my state of mind. I choose to never let anyone's betrayals cause me to lose my kindness, compassion, and love for any other living being. That's the choice I made. Though I'm choosing the spiritual path of forgiveness, I certainly don't live in denial about evil or abuse. I see it. I know it's out there. But I can't control it and I certainly don't want it to have any control over me. I find that working to have a forgiving spirit, seeking joy, and making an honest attempt to find suffering, pain, and abuse before it overcomes us are essential tools in recovering we have to dig our way out of the shame, rage, denial, and trust issues and heal our lives.

The Book On Forgiveness

Empathy and Understanding in Forgiveness

There is only one theory here, hardly enough to claim for it the ability to explain everything, much less to make it into forgiveness. However, this theory does include three things that seem important in forgiveness. First, there is no evidence that forgiving leads to recovery without explanation. Any motivator of forgiving's relationship with psychological wellbeing that does not consider the act of forgiveness part of the equation is like a form of physics that would start and stop discussing the movement of an object with the first and last actions of the object itself. Second, for debate, within person variables play a bigger role than do between person variables in discussions of forgiveness and its consequences. We seem to reason about our own relationships. And, when we find our private conclusions about relationships under siege, our behaviour is not as pro-social as good communal friendship would have it be.

Empathy and sympathy are direct, personal understandings of the pain and suffering of others, tolerating differences from self, tolerating the fact that the differences are such, that sympathy and empathy cannot replace love. Yet, showing empathy and sympathy is a good action that can help forgive. A secular approach, within the confines simply of psychological aspects, echoes the humanity echoed from religious teachings. Such reference to religion-free debate was neither the start of the literature on the relevance of social support, for instance, to forgiveness, nor was it novel insight. Saying it here is important, however, and should be repeated in the future, because secular debate does seem to sometimes work at odds with religion, rather than being separate from religion when it comes to interpersonal relationships.

The Book On Forgiveness

Inspiring Others

After my friend's son was killed, her fiancé built a memorial for DeAndre where he died, which caused a lot of friction with DeAndre's mother, Victoria. When Victoria brought her to court to sue for possession of DeAndre's body because she wanted to move him to her city, the judge denied my request. Victoria was awarded possession of DeAndre's body and a funeral was scheduled for the next Saturday. The next day, the memorial that her fiancé had

constructed for DeAndre was vandalised and no longer stood. All of the parent pain that DeAndre and I had been feeling for the last fifteen years was taken out on that memorial in just a few seconds.

When my friend's fiancé told her that he wanted to rebuild the memorial that had stood for half of DeAndre's life, she taught him the process of forgiveness is one in which there are steps: seeing the person outside of now and where they were. He said, "I know you want everyone to get along, but I am tired of just taking the pain and doing nothing about it." I will always remember my fiancé saying, "If it makes you feel better, I'll forgive Victoria. You are right. It was not her fault. But, I would like to do this for her." I called it "a project of love". Her response to him was "If she is allowed to have a funeral to say goodbye to her son tomorrow, she would rebuild the memorial, a place where all of DeAndre's friends can come to say goodbye." In her heart of hearts, she did want to be the "better person" and make a "positive difference" no matter how hard it was. My friend found the root of herself then and she will always want to respond in a way to make both DeAndre and her son happy for the young man who forgave. Large numbers of her son's friends believe that DeAndre's spirit lives there. The new memorial has him embracing the word "KING." My friend's son's friends believe that if you stand in front of the cross, you can hear him speak.

The Book On Forgiveness

Sharing a Forgiveness Journey

For most people, it's a very private thing. We don't walk around asking people if they've forgiven someone today... should we? No, I don't think so. But there is a tremendous power in sharing your story - both for the one sharing and for those that hear it. Perhaps there is a place for a very public celebration of forgiveness. There are many celebrities who have shared their forgiveness journey and even some who are making it their life's work to help others through their own personal knowledge of what forgiveness is. There remains, however, many people who live in communities or in circles of friends and families who have not heard of or experienced the true power of forgiveness. So many people are motivated too often by anger, revenge, and guilt. Think right now of the people you know - friends, family, neighbours, and co-workers, that walk with bitterness, anger, and revenge. For many of them, their road has not led them to forgiveness.

Conclusion

In conclusion, the chapter underscores that the transformative power of forgiveness is within everyone's reach and embracing it can lead to a deeply fulfilling life. Forgiveness is a profound act that allows you to heal from the wounds of the past, release lingering bitterness, and open your heart to love and joy. It's a journey of personal liberation, where letting go of grievances and resentments frees you from the shackles of negative emotions.

Achieving this transformation requires a conscious decision to forgive, which is often challenging but immensely rewarding. It involves a commitment to replace anger and hurt with understanding and compassion, not just for others but for yourself as well. By doing so, you create space for positive emotions and experiences to enter your life, fostering a sense of peace and well-being.

Surrounding yourself with positive influences and seeking out good experiences are crucial steps in this journey. These choices help reinforce your commitment to forgiveness and provide a supportive environment that nurtures personal growth. The chapter suggests that by forgiving others, you also invite forgiveness into your own life, leading to healthier relationships and a more vibrant inner life.

You can achieve this transformation by taking deliberate steps to practice forgiveness daily. This may involve reflecting on past grievances, acknowledging your feelings, and then consciously choosing to release them. It might also mean seeking reconciliation or simply finding peace in letting go. The result is a life filled with deeper connections, a sense of freedom, and a newfound appreciation for the beauty of the present moment.

Ultimately, the message is clear: forgiveness is not just an act of kindness towards others, but a gift you give to yourself. It's a path to reclaiming your joy, nurturing your soul, and living a life that is rich with love and fulfilment. You, too, have the power to transform your life through forgiveness, achieving a state of inner peace and contentment that radiates out into every aspect of your existence.

The Book On Forgiveness

About the Author:

Shalini Mittal is a distinguished Senior Broadcaster at All India Radio with 30 years of experience. She is a versatile A-grade Drama Artist, National Commentator for VVIP programmes, and Graded Music Artist. As part of the sports coverage team, she has reported on the Asian Games in Incheon, South Korea, and the National Games in Gujarat and Goa. Recognised with multiple awards, including thrice by UNICEF and twice for best production, Shalini is also a Covid Immunisation Champion. She has led diverse broadcasting activities, notably as Channel Head of FM Rainbow for six years, and has contributed significantly to prestigious programs like "Mann ki Baat."

CHAPTER 24

The magic of forgiveness

FORGIVENESS

Dr. P. Prabhavathy

Dr. Vichitra Sivaji

Dr. V. Brinda Shree

Mrs. Y.R. Sareena Angelin

Dr. Parin Somani

The desire to be forgiven, to forgive, and be at peace with the past is something that all people share. Not one of us is above doing something wrong or facing hard times—they are woven into the human experience. From the petty and painful, to the significant and tragic, we all have received a wrong, suffered from it, and watched its remnants ripple for years later. However, "desiring to be at peace, and to get right with everything that is wrong, is actually a step in the right direction." This simple beauty is forgiveness. Generally, forgiveness is vital to our growth and happiness as we undergo the torchers of gaining respect, success, and happiness. As individuals grow up, they learn to forgive others, build relationships and improve themselves. This essay will discuss forgiveness as a subject for personal growth based on personal experiences and the lessons learned.

Personal Growth and Forgiveness

We have all been wronged at some time. We all know how anger, bitterness, and resentment dominate our thoughts and feelings when we hold grudges. That rage can be exhausting. But we would rather hoard all our upsets than grant amnesty and approval to those who have wounded us. Why? Because it's natural to feel anger and hate, to allow resentment to consume you, and to punish those who have slighted you. We still have the ability to choose compassion, understanding, warmth, and saying "... but I release you." While we won't be able to forget the infraction, we'll be able to share an atmosphere of reconciliation, respect, and even thankfulness with someone who is still around. It's a heavy lift, but we're all worth it.

While and when we were physically and emotionally healing from our indignities, we were given a few motivations to strategies on what we would do if we ever met those who transgressed against us. We've often pondered what it would have been like if it were us, if we had made the same choices. It's a lesson for us to study, a road trip of learning from personal experience. We had become aware of how it was so easy to judge and punish someone when you had the moral kindness to "be in the right," but how tough and irrelevant it was to show love and comfort to someone who had wronged you. Our individual experiences have taught us the moral power forgiveness held.

Lessons Learnt From Experiences

One of the most valuable things we can learn from challenging situations that have hurt us is the power of empathy. Many of us might have been in the shoes of those who benefited from the act of forgiveness, but some of us might identify more with those who seek to be forgiven or have to cope with the consequences. Regardless, understanding someone else's point of view and validating their emotions is one of the sincerest forms of kindness and one of the most valuable lessons we can take away from this. Growing is often an integral component of the forgiveness equation. Coming to terms with the fact that everyone is capable of making the same mistake can be enlightening and help to let go of any frustration. Being willing to change your behaviour and asking for forgiveness is essential to the process.

The Book On Forgiveness

Patience can also be an important part of letting go of any lingering anger – especially if the situation is ongoing.

Forgiveness is such an important process because it gives people the opportunity to self-reflect and think about how they contribute to a relationship. Admitting to your share of the blame is helpful for disarming the other person, making it less likely that the situation will escalate further. Many of the stories highlight the possibility for rebuilding trust once forgiveness is granted. We actively hold onto resentment and anger.

Once we can start to let go of our negative emotions, it gives us a chance to show up and work on the relationships that we care about keeping. There can be positives to come out of any relationship crisis that leads to forgiveness, especially if the other person has taken the time to reflect on their behaviour and offer an apology. Embracing forgiveness as a strength rather than a weakness enables people to feel liberated and disengaged from the person who did the wronging. For those concerned with equity in the universe, the act of forgiving can feel self-sacrificial, but the true nature of forgiveness is detailed by the forgiveness stories above.

Releasing Resentment for Inner Peace

Numerous individuals in my research discussed emotional responses to holding onto resentment and the importance of letting it go. When life deals you a tragedy, when you find yourself in court or something else, if you don't release resentment, well you're never going to be at ease. Resentment grows in you, intensifies, and comes out in odd ways. Letting feelings fester can worsen a traumatic event by harbouring negative emotions. It's true at first you get resentment, which slowly turns into hate. And hate spreads through your whole body, and oh, hate does hurt. Cause then you're all tied up, you're like a pretzel. Resentment is known to have various negative impacts from feelings of discomfort to physical illness.

Letting go prompts the release of anger and allows for inner peace to be gained. Shellie told me that the act of letting go was sacrificial in nature, and that she had to make a conscious decision to give up resentment.

"Because you're not angry anymore, and you know when you think you've given away everything that was once yours, which isn't really yours, well, but in your mind, then things are just so much better. You can smile. It's like hey, I'm over here! Go ahead." In releasing the burden of resentment, one finally comes to a place of freedom and serenity. Rebuilding trust and relationships through forgiveness. Forgiveness is responsible for restoring trust in organisations; without it, an organisation may face a loss of integrity and a reduction in value. Forgiveness is noted in relation to spirituality and increased organisational commitment, having a positive impact in mediating relationships while reversing the negative effect of stress on these relationships.

In relationships, forgiveness is important in improving positive emotions and it is an indication of being "cheating immune" when one's investment in a cooperatively structured social system has been threatened or harmed.

Forgiveness as a Path to Healing

Forgiving someone is hard enough when the person is alive and can ask for forgiveness, but it's significantly more difficult when the person is dead, or you just can't see them anymore. Carrying a grudge is like carrying a heavy sack of pain around all day. If you forgive someone for hurting you, you are letting go of that heavy sack. When you carry a grudge, it's like you are taking poison, and waiting for the other person to die. You can't have a healthy relationship when others' behaviour is controlling you. Forgiveness helps a person recover emotionally from loss, helps us find and develop inner freedom and freedom of thought, and it comes from a part of the brain that seeks only your own best outcome.

Our views combined

Through our combined personal experiences, we each embarked on a different path and arrived at a destination that suited us in different ways. There seems to be something powerful about having the capacity to let go and reject retribution.

When we listen to some of the stories of people who hurt others, we are also struck by the guilt and pain they continue to experience. Forgiveness seems to offer an alternative signpost that invites these people to take the pathway of healing and hope. Embedding forgiving actions or postures is hard. It is not a quick fix or remedy - it is a slow transformative process. For those thinking about the big stuff, we encourage you to embrace it as a journey - an inner dialogue that carries a powerful message about hope, personal journey, dignity and empathy for self and others.

Each person has a unique story and experience of forgiveness and victimisation. There are also vital commonalities, and, if we tried to summarise some of those, the process of forgiveness likely saved our lives, mental health and even souls. Hate can be so incapacitating and cannot be ignored

We believe that Self-compassion is the force that supports us in forgiveness, the ultimate salve for our wounds and the purest defence against anger, which descends unbidden with any rise in the waterline. Compassion bathes that anger in empathy, to reveal our own humanity. We're all vulnerable. It's one of the deepest truths we can know. We are temporarily able-bodied, our loved ones are mortal, and we are ultimately powerless to determine the future. Compassion for ourselves brings us the balance we need to feel sorry for the shooter whose wounds are so deep he could not see the souls of those he felt the need to kill.

When a moment flashes with beauty, we fan ourselves with a mental flick of compassion inside ourselves, for ourselves, for swiftly pinning to our diaspora of heartache. Empathy harnesses our compassion; it is the amalgamation of all experiences, good and bad, that allows us to anticipate an outcome in the conversation or argument swirling around us. "Meaning is to be earned through action," philosopher Myles Brand said, "and action stems from thought that has been educated by experience." We use experience to sift out assumptions in empathy to bring an honest truth to the surface. The easiest way to do that, is to be compassionate towards yourself. Enfold yourself in empathy and cradle your hurts as you drop them, one by one, healed at last, into the forgiving light.

The emotional growth that is achieved when we forgive another comes not only during the process of forgiving but also as it becomes a way of being in the world. When done properly, forgiveness is an active process. It requires you to face the worst thing that has ever happened to you, acknowledge your pain, and move through it in order to move on. When we do this, we recognise that it is not our emotional energy that should be taken up with the actions of another individual. If people who do bad things cause us to feel and act hatefully, they have succeeded in perpetuating the hate. Same energy - new direction.

Our Message of Hope and Healing

To forgive others is to make a choice, but most people realise that by forgiving and moving forward, a positive message is also left behind. As adults age, the experiences from the past also age and mature, and sometimes they blend with the background. Although experiences are like impurities, people are able to move beyond them and not remain embittered. At times, these impurities still reflect those times that are in the past and are held onto, but a choice of forgiveness helps us rise above them and leave a positive message of hope and healing.

Very few people who go through terrible life events can easily forgive and let go. Most circumstances like this greatly affect people's lives. They revert to their old lifestyles. But when one does forgive, they take the people around them by surprise. Their courage and resilience give hope to the survivors who witnessed their healing. The world needs to understand that forgiveness emerges from among us and that resilience stalks the soil of our country. Sometimes we need only be brave enough to love one another.

The Book On Forgiveness

About the Author(s):

Dr. P. Prabhavathy

Dr. P. Prabhavathy is a Professor of English in the Department of Science and Humanities at KGiSL, Coimbatore, Tamil Nadu, India. She has authored technical textbooks, workbooks, and reference books, and contributed articles, chapters, and research papers for international conferences, journals, and magazines. Dr. Prabhavathy serves as a speaking and written examiner for BULATS – ESOL Examinations, British Council, Cambridge Assessment, and Evaluation, EBEK. She has received numerous awards and was recently recognised as an AICTE-certified UHV Mentor. Her extensive contributions to academia and assessment highlight her dedication to education and linguistic excellence.

Dr. Vichitra Sivaji

Dr. Vichitra Sivaji specialises in English Language Teaching. She earned her Ph.D. from Bharathiar University in 2014 and completed her M.Phil. from Madurai Kamaraj University in 2007. She holds a PG Diploma in TEFL/TESOL, specialising in Teaching Young Learners and Business English. With 25 years of teaching and research experience, she is a life member of ELTAI and has contributed to The International Library of Poetry. She has 7 years of international teaching experience and has been recognised for

her dedication to teaching. Her interests include ELT and integrating technology with communication skills.

Mrs. Y.R. Sareena Angelin

Mrs. Y.R. Sareena Angelin is an Assistant Professor in the Department of English at Adithya Institute of Technology, Coimbatore. A native of Tamil Nadu, she earned her M.A. in English Literature from Nirmala College, Coimbatore, and her M.A. and M.Phil in Translation from Madurai Kamarajar University. Additionally, she has studied Psychology & Counselling and is currently pursuing an MBA in Human Resources at Bharathiyar University. With a special interest in educational psychology and innovative teaching methods, Mrs. Angelin has been teaching since June 2010. She also holds a Diploma in Personality Development from Cambridge University. Her future plans include developing new educational methodologies to enhance human ethics in Indian education.

Dr. V. Brinda Shree

Dr. V. Brinda Shree, deeply passionate about English literature, earned her Doctorate in English from Bharathiar University, Coimbatore, specializing in Indo-Anglican Literature. Born and raised in Mysore, she currently serves as the Head of the Department of English at Dr. N. G. P. Institute of Technology, Coimbatore, Tamil Nadu. With over 14 years of teaching experience, Dr. Brinda has facilitated undergraduate and postgraduate students across Arts, Commerce, Science, MBA, Architecture, and Engineering disciplines. A Cambridge English Examiner

for BEC Examinations, she has also undergone training with the British Council. She has presented over 49 research papers and authored a book chapter, and has presented at international venues including Lincoln University, Malaysia.

Prof. Dr. Parin Somani

Prof. Dr. Parin Somani is CEO and Director of LOSD (www.losd.co.uk), a distinguished Academic Scholar, three times TEDx Speaker, and Author of 21 books. To inspire individuals to reach their true potential, she has won Mrs. Universe 2022, Mrs. World 2022 in Thailand, Mrs. BritAsian 2021 in London, Mrs. India 2021, Mrs. Universe International 2021, and Mrs. India Global 2021. She has been recognised in numerous World Record Books like the Guinness World Records and was one of the Lead Editors of 'The Thickest Book in the World.' Her passion for lifelong learning and helping global societies has led her to achieve 2 Academic and 6 Honorary Doctorates and numerous multi-international awards. She is immensely grateful for all her honours, and she has been invited to deliver keynote speeches at conferences at Cambridge, Harvard and Oxford University, and many more. Her global travels to 127 countries have enabled her to contribute to her main areas of focus: education, women empowerment, and youth development.

As we reach the conclusion of "The Book On Forgiveness," it is important to reflect on the profound journeys shared within these pages. The twenty-seven authors have generously opened their hearts, offering us a glimpse into their personal experiences and insights with forgiveness within the twenty-four chapters in the year 2024. Their stories have taken us through moments of deep pain and suffering, but also to places of immense strength, resilience, and healing.

Forgiveness, as we have seen, is not a linear path but a complex and often challenging journey. It requires us to confront our deepest wounds and to extend compassion not only to those who have wronged us but also to ourselves. Through these narratives, we have learned that forgiveness is an ongoing process, one that demands patience, persistence, and a willingness to let go of anger and resentment.

The lessons embedded in these stories are universal. They remind us that forgiveness is a powerful act of liberation, freeing us from the chains of past hurts and opening the door to healing and personal growth. It allows us to rebuild relationships, find inner peace, and approach life with renewed purpose and understanding.

As you close this book, we invite you to carry the insights and wisdom shared by these authors into your own life. Reflect on the stories that resonated most with you and consider how you might apply their lessons to your own journey. Whether you are grappling with forgiveness in your personal relationships, seeking to heal from past traumas, or striving to cultivate greater self-compassion, remember that you are not alone. The experiences and reflections in this book are a testament to the shared human capacity for forgiveness and transformation.

May "The Book On Forgiveness" serve as a lasting source of inspiration and guidance. As you move forward, may you find the courage to forgive, the strength to heal, and the grace to embrace each new day with a heart full of compassion.

Together, let us build a world where forgiveness is not just an act, but a way of being a world where we can all find peace and renewal.

Thank you for joining us on this journey.

23
POSITIVE CHANGE
MAKERS IN THE WORLD 2023
24 PROMINENT PERSONALITIES IN THE WORLD 2024
LOSD
24
PROMINENT
PERSONALITIES
IN THE WORLD 2024
DR. PARIN SOMANI
Dreaming,
Seeing and
Believing...
Manifest
Inner
Beauty
PART 1
MANIFEST INNER BEAUTY (PART 1)

THE HEALING BLUEPRINT: UNLOCKING THE SECRETS TO PHYSICAL, EMOTIONAL, AND SPIRITUAL WELL-BEING
The
Healing
Blueprint
Unlocking the Secrets to Physical,
Emotional, and Spiritual Well-Being
LEADERSHIP
LIMITS LEADING
RISING BEYO
TODAY FOR TOMORROW'S W
Prof. Dr Parin Somani
MANIFEST
HEALTHY
WEIGHT LOSS:
A Transformative Journey: Part - 1
PROF. DR. PARIN SOMANI | DR. BOLA BENSON | DR. MAGGIE BENSON

9 798889 610586